CONSTRUCTION
CLEANUP

D1193424

More Books by Don Aslett

FOR PROFESSIONAL CLEANERS:

Cleaning Up for a Living
The Professional Cleaner's
    Personal Handbook
How to Upgrade & Motivate
    Your Cleaning Crews
Construction Cleanup
The Brighter Side of the Broom
Professional Cleaner's Clip Art

AUTOBIOGRAPHY:

How I Swept My Way to the Top:
    The Don Aslett Story

BUSINESS BOOKS:

Barnyard to Boardroom:
    Business Basics
DONE! (How to Have a
    48-Hour Day)
The Office Clutter Cure
Keeping Work Simple
How to Be #1 With Your Boss
Speak Up! A Step-by-Step Guide to
    Powerful Public Speeches
A Toilet Cleaner's Attitude

OTHER BOOKS ON CLEANING:

No Time to Clean!
Is There Life After Housework?
Do I Dust or Vacuum First?
The Cleaning Encyclopedia
Don Aslett's Clean in a Minute
Don Aslett's Stainbuster's Bible

Make Your House Do the
    Housework
HELP! Around the House
Who Says It's a Woman's Job
    to Clean?
Wood Floor Care
Pet Clean-Up Made Easy
Painting Without Fainting

BOOKS ON DECLUTTERING AND PERSONAL ORGANIZATION:

Clutter's Last Stand
For Packrats Only
Clutter Free! Finally & Forever
The Office Clutter Cure
Weekend Makeover (Lose 200 Lbs.
    This Weekend)
DONE! (How to Have a
    48-Hour Day)
How to Handle 1,000 Things
    at Once
Dejunk Live! (Audio CD)

OTHER:

How Successful People Keep Their
    Lives Out of the Toilet

WRITING BOOKS:

Get Organized, Get Published!
How to Write and Sell Your
    First Book
You Can... You Should...
    Write Poetry

CONSTRUCTION CLEANUP

A GUIDE TO AN EXCITING AND PROFITABLE CLEANING SPECIALTY

By DON ASLETT

AMERICA'S #1 CLEANING EXPERT

MARSH CREEK PRESS

Construction Cleanup

Copyright © 1997 by Don Aslett.

Updated edition 2011.

Published by

MARSH CREEK PRESS

Marsh Creek Press
PO Box 700
Pocatello, Idaho 83204
Phone 208-232-3535
Fax 208-235-5481
www.aslett.com
ISBN 0-937750-17-4
978-0-937750-17-9

To purchase this book in quantity at a discount, contact the publisher above.

Editor: Carol Cartaino
Production Manager: Tobi Alexander
Illustrator: Kerry Otteson

Construction Cleanup

is the process of removing all traces of
construction dust, dirt, and debris from
new or remodeled structures and leaving
them totally clean—soil- and spot-free and
ready for occupancy.

About the Author

The man who went door to door cleaning houses to work his way through college, and more than fifty years of hard-earned experience later, is now the head of one of the nation's leading facility services companies. His company, Varsity Contractors, Inc., is now an 80+ million dollar operation in all 50 states and Canada.

Don Aslett isn't just America's #1 Cleaning Expert, he's everyone's favorite cleaner. For five decades now he's been teaching professional cleaners and homemakers across the country how to clean faster and better, and even more amazing—keeping them smiling all the while.

He burst on the national scene in 1981 with his first big best-seller, **Is There Life After Housework?** a book that is now almost a household word. For the first time ever, it brought the tools and techniques of the professionals to the aid of the home cleaner.

Aslett has done more than three dozen equally popular books since, bringing his refreshingly down-to-earth and original approach to not only cleaning but decluttering and personal organization, secrets of business success, low-maintenance home design, and how to be a better speaker.

His books for the professional cleaner—and would-be professional—include everything from a complete guide to running your own successful cleaning business, to guides to profitable specialties within the industry, and to how to motivate your cleaning crews. His books are perennial best-sellers—they've sold more than three million copies to date—and they've been featured by major book clubs and translated into eight languages.

CONTENTS

INTRODUCTION

My company, Varsity Contractors, Inc., did its first construction cleanup job in 1958, for Western Electric. Following that we did new homes, apartments, schools, resorts, parks, communication buildings, office buildings, large complexes, and huge hotels like the MGM Grand in Nevada. We cleaned up after remodeling and renovation and brand-new construction, all sizes of jobs, from 300 square feet to 3,000,000 square feet. We cleaned in the dead of winter and the suffocating heat of summer; for mean, dishonest, and poorly organized contractors and for the nicest, most honest, and efficient companies around. We made money, lost money, and often worked hard for weeks just to come out even. Some jobs were wonderful, some pure misery—but most were well worth doing. We remember all of them, kept records, and have collected over 50 years of input from numerous other construction cleanup specialty contractors as well. All of this is condensed and presented in this volume. It is not the complete or final word on the subject, but hundreds of little hows, whats, whens, and whys to help make construction cleanup easier, faster, and more profitable.

Don Aslett, Founder
Varsity Contractors, Inc.

2

CONSTRUCTION CLEANUP:

A good place to jump into the cleaning business and clean up!

WHY?

 Construction (new and remodeling) is always going on, everywhere! That means two big things: 1. There has to be some kind of cleanup! 2. There is money available to pay for it!

 The jobs here can range from a single small private residence to a 3,000,000-square-foot building or a 30-apartment building complex spread over 25 acres.

Construction is a good ground floor or start-up job for launching your cleaning career. Small companies have every advantage big, famous companies do on these jobs. Experience comes quickly as most construction cleaning needs are similar.

 Construction cleanup is not complicated. The procedures involved are relatively simple and require a minimum of training. Patience, persistence, and personality mean more here than technical knowledge or sheer skill. Anyone can learn to do construction cleanup well and profitably if they have the ability to work and stick to it.

 Construction cleanup requires a minimum of equipment and supplies as compared to other cleaning industry specialties.

 Construction cleanup can be a one- or two-person operation or performed by a 10- or 25-person crew, depending on the number and size of the units and the move-in or selling schedule.

 90% of the surfaces, fixtures, and furnishings you will be working with are NEW and thus easy to clean and make look good.

 This also means that the quality of any job of construction cleanup is easily charted and measured, thus eliminating most of the arguing, blaming, and arbitration involved in other types of cleaning assignments.

 There is job security here, too. Once you work for a general contractor or facility boss, if you do well, THEY WILL HIRE YOU AGAIN. They are pretty loyal and likely to give you all of their work from then on.

What is construction cleanup?

The cleaning up that needs to be done after a building is built, renovated, remodeled, or repaired, to make the structure and premises bright, shiny, sanitary, and 100% attractive for that big opening day. It needs to be done in homes, apartments, schools, and industrial and commercial buildings of every kind.

WHO CAN BENEFIT FROM THIS BOOK?

1. CONSTRUCTION CONTRACTORS
who do their own cleanup.

2. OWNERS OF BUILDINGS AND FACILITIES
if they choose to do their own cleanup.

3. REALTORS
who might be in the middle.

4. CLEANING CONTRACTORS
and crews who do this for a living.

5. INDIVIDUALS
who have (or would like to have) a part-time cleaning business.

Finding Construction Cleanup Jobs

They are busy, those builders, so don't wait for them to find you in the Yellow Pages. They welcome and appreciate a selection of willing cleaning contractors. Here are some "hustle" principles.

1. Subscribe to and follow the local construction newsletter (with its record of bids and permits).

2. When you see a lot being graded, find the builders.

3. Look for signs advertising future development.

4. Look for buildings being torn down.

5. Join an association of local building owners and managers and advertise.

6. Include "Construction Cleanup" in the lettering on your trucks and brochures.

7. Watch for new malls, banks, and office remodeling.

8. Check with banks and other construction-financing institutions.

9. Contact local construction companies.

10. Subscribe to local business magazines or newspapers.

11. Check with Realtors, developers, and architectural firms.

12. Cultivate and carry over all of your present loyal clients.

13. Put up postcards, brochures, even posters at building supply stores, lumberyards, etc.

Let's Make the Last Thing the First Thing:

HOW TO PRICE AND GET PAID

Many of you bought this book just to learn how to price (the rest of you are willing to figure out by trial and error). If you expect this chapter to give you ALL the secrets of exact, perfect pricing, I'd return the book and learn pricing by trial and error, too. You will find lots of direction, wisdom, and guidance here however, as well as examples of how "we" (we other construction cleanup people) price construction cleanup.

The glitch is:

1. No two jobs are the same.

2. No two contractors will leave a unit the same.

3. We don't all have the same equipment, experience, and speed.

4. No two owners or builders are the same. Some are easy to work with; others you'll never please.

5. Help and labor costs are not the same everywhere.

6. Employee availability is never predictable; there is either a surplus or slim pickin's in workers.

7. No weather conditions (even in the same season and same area) are ever the same.

8. No two cities' ordinances for garbage, parking, noise, etc., are the same.

9. Once you submit a price, you must honor it.

You will learn some aspects of pricing by trial and error to fit your area, the local economic conditions, and your experience and speed, but if you follow these guidelines your learning should be pleasant and profitable.

An important precaution— LOOK FIRST

There is something you cannot control, but you can allow for, and that is the <u>condition the contractor and subcontractors leave the building in</u>.

If you take on a job where the contractor and subs have left the place new but smeared, piled, dripped, slopped, and spilled on, and there is trash all over, it can double your time and trips, and the supplies needed. Hopefully, after one disheveled job, you'll learn to not walk into another bad one. Cleaning a "clean" newly constructed counter or bathroom is unbelievably different from cleaning one with sheet rock mud, plaster, contact cement, ink marks, and wrappings all over. This is why you <u>always look at a job before bidding</u>. If it's a slob job, bid it higher! If it's almost perfect, you can sure be competitive. So…

The first rule of pricing is:

VISIT THE SITE!

Look over the units/building you are going to clean! Don't bid from plans! We all love to look like big wheels walking around with plans under our arms, but plans don't tell what kind of hardware or wainscoting there is, or how sloppy the subs have been, etc. Go look! Always! Before you pick up a pencil, take a quick walk around the place and get a quick overview of what you are pricing—why, where, when, with whom, etc.

> **REMEMBER, like people, all places are different. Always look at and walk the site. Don't bid from a set of plans or unseen square footage figures.**

Then:

WRITE IT DOWN!

WRITE DOWN any questions, concerns, or doubts you have about a job, any phase of it. Write them down in enough detail so that after you have reviewed these things with the client there is absolutely no misunderstanding of the amount, terms, what will be done—how, where, and when (including a time limit beyond which you will not be responsible for redos, or a limit on the number of recleanings of any area for the price agreed upon). Don't rely on your memory, or try to handle this by comments or conversation alone. WRITE IT DOWN—this shows you are paying attention, it makes a record, and defuses arbitration situations should they crop up in the future.

"Should You Take It On?" Here's a CHECKLIST

Before you start any counting, measuring, adding, subtracting, or multiplying, this checklist (like the ones pilots use before takeoff) will keep you out of trouble. Remember, figuring is the EASIEST PART OF bidding. It is the preliminary investigation that really counts! Not only does this assist you in pricing, and in getting the job, but also in obtaining the confidence of the owner/builder. If you can't find out all of the following, then that is the first "caution" sign.

"Should You Take It On?" CHECKLIST

Location: Where the job is, is critical. It may be too far away, or right in a crowded downtown with no parking within 50 blocks. It could be in the middle of a desert or on the peak of Pine Cliff mountain. Travel cost and time, parking, etc., are big factors in costing. Some construction cleanup jobs will end up with 29 hours of actual work and 15 hours of travel time (between you and your employees). You could price the square footage and time of a job perfectly, yet if it takes eight trips of fifty miles each, at 40 cents a mile travel expense, the vehicle cost alone for the job would be $180. Your and your employees' time spent in travel could be thirty hours at $10, and there is another $240. This means that just getting to where you need to be to do the work will cost $400. And this might only be a $600 or $700 job. If the job is a block from your home or shop, all of that expense is eliminated. "Too far" often means "too bad."

Size of job: Are you cleaning one house or the whole development tract, one apartment or 700? Often setup, bidding, equipment, supplies, rentals, billing, etc., cost about the same for a $500 job as for a $5000 job. The constant fixed costs are about the same for a small job as for a big one, so there is an economy of scale to be considered here. The more costs can be spread out the better; that's why you can give a price break or discount on volume.

Working hours: When can you do the job? How soon after the builders finish do the tenants or owner move in? If times are real tight, weather or shipping are problems, etc., it can cause lost days, and you will be the one "at fault." You may be sued or not paid when it wasn't your fault at all. Will you be working days, or nights, or weekends? (Remember that at least half of all the places you might need to go for supplies are closed on Saturday and Sunday.)

Liability risk and safety: How high are the windows, light fixtures, and ceilings, how high are the stair railings? Worker's Comp coverage can be up to 60% of your payroll dollars if there are great heights involved. Since your people will be doing all the work, it will affect all of the payroll, even the vacuumers. Will it be hazardous getting to and from work?

Weather factors: What will it be like when they finish the structure and call you to clean it up? Too cold? Too hot? Wind blowing, snowing, raining constantly? All of these factors influence the production rate and the quality of a cleaning job—no matter how fast or spirited you are, weather can and will affect your end result. You cannot control the weather, but if you have a clue as to what it might be, you can prepare for it and bid for it.

Initial investment: How much money or equipment is needed for the job? You might get a super onetime shot at a $1000 roof repair job that you can do in one day. However, if you need $2000 worth of equipment to do it and your Worker's Comp insurance increases to $25 per hour for the rest of the year… I wouldn't touch it!

Is the money good? Do they pay? When? How?

Personality: Who you work for is almost as important as what you are doing. If the client is a jerk, your best work probably won't please him and he will speak evil of you forevermore. Check the references of those you might work for: Are they stable and well established? Do they pay their bills? Are they reasonable, or complaining constantly, etc.?

"Should You Take It On?" CHECKLIST *continued...*

Good   Un-   Bad

Access/occupancy: Who is going to be there when you are cleaning? Are the tenants going to be moving in, will there be any last-minute painting or HVAC people tromping over your waxed floors, etc.? Can you get to all the areas you need to clean when you show up, or will they be installing computers in one room so it is locked all the time, so you have to come back later? Will there be others at the site that you have to work around forever? People in the way can easily double your cleaning time and hurt your quality a lot too! Will there be convenient access to utilities?

Security: How safe will your equipment and supplies be during your working time and during the night? Can you leave your ladder and extractor and scaffolding and chemicals there? Is the area locked? Who has the key? Can vandals graffiti the area right behind you? What is the union situation? Any potential picketing or hassles? Could you get in the middle of a dispute and get terminated by politics?

Management: Do you have the horses to do the job? Enough supervisory personnel and actual cleaners, for that matter, to round up for the job? If you don't and can't get them economically, I'd let even a fat job go by. Strain yourself if it is necessary but don't bid and take work without the management and muscle to perform it.

Review records: If you've done other construction cleanup jobs, review the old job sheets and billings. You'll be amazed how much information will present itself when you do. You might find tiny things you left out last time, or things they loved or hated that can be incorporated into or omitted on this bid.

For any of the items in this list checked "Bad" or "Unknown," go back and get an answer or solution before you bid.

If only one single factor in the checklist suggests significant risk, that may be reason enough to pass on the job. Some of the topics in this checklist may be mentioned or discussed again in other sections of this book. Many of them apply to more than one part of finding, getting, doing, and billing jobs. They are in there again for a reason, to stress how important they are to a good, profitable cleanup job.

The Different Methods of Pricing

Of all cleaning work, construction cleanup is the most difficult to bid, because of the uncertainties of what condition the contractors will leave the building in. "Broom clean" (a term we will often hear in construction cleanup discussions and contracts) has 72 definitions, so let's cover all possibilities: Per hour, per square foot, per unit, and per bid.

PER HOUR PRICING

Ultimately, payment per hour is the most fair if you work fast and hard, and the client pays a fair rate. Then no matter what needs to be done, how many times, and for how long, it is easy to figure out how much to charge. You will be slightly more under the client's control in this situation, but SAFER because construction cleanup has its risks. If you use this method you need to:

1. Establish a fair, agreed-upon hourly rate. (Remember fair is a two-way street.)

2. Make, and follow, a firm outline of exactly what the client wants done.

3. Document your hours accurately.

Let's look at each of these in more detail now.

1 ESTABLISHING YOUR HOURLY RATE

A realistic hourly rate often sounds high. This is a hurdle, but remember that not just wages, but expenses, overhead, insurance, and extras all have to be included in your rate. Then, too, you often have people and locations with differing hourly rates in a job, but the client wants a firm rate.

Here's an example of what your calculations here might include:

Your worker .... $8.00 per hr.

FICA, insurance, etc...... $1.80

Overhead.................... $1.50

Equipment/supplies......... $.50

Profit.......................... $2.40

$14.20

So $14 or $15 an hour is what you'll have to charge. It sounds high when the minimum wage is $6.25, but you are the one who will be doing the work, so you decide the rate.

You'll find that with an hourly rate, you'll need to have consistent, high quality workers on the job site. If you have any slow pokes, drones or slackers the supervisor will be after you. There IS and always will be a barrier to hourly charging—people perceive cleaners as "low paid," not in the class of carpenters, masons, painters, and the like. They think of cleaning as worth "maid wages," so a healthy rate will be hard to sell until the contractor knows you. I feel you should make a $2-$4 PROFIT per hour on your people and pay yourself around $20 per hour if you work on the job yourself. Once your rate is established don't let them haggle you down.

2 MAKE AND FOLLOW A FIRM OUTLINE

Start a cleanup TO DO LIST with the client when the contract first begins (put a "to do" box before and "done" box after each task on the list).

Keep the list visible—always.

Have an "initial" box, too, so that when additions or deletions are made, the initials of the authorizing person can be recorded.

Keep the list current and agreed-upon throughout the whole job.

3 DOCUMENT YOUR HOURS

Have every person on the job list their hours, every day: the date, the times they logged in and out, a brief description of their duties, and their name or signature. I wouldn't display this publicly.

Be fair

A good deal in construction cleanup means a good deal for the owner, the builder, and you.

Be fair! There is always a tomorrow. Building and remodeling never quit and fair pricing is one of the best ways to get work and stay in business.

PER UNIT PRICING

Per unit pricing only works when you have a consistent number and size of units or rooms, with more or less the same duties to be done in each, like hotels, motels, condos, apartments, classrooms, and some office buildings or tract homes. You simply figure the time, cost, equipment, and effort needed to completely clean one of the units (either by doing one or bidding it) and then set that price as "the" cost for each unit.

For example you agree on the rate of $92 per apartment. The complex has 100 units, so your bid is $9200 total.

This type of pricing has benefits for both you and the contractor.

THEY know the exact cost and there are no surprises.

YOUR duties are consistent and contained—which means a much easier job to run and track accountability on.

I like per unit bidding because it has flexibility and challenge—a chance to exercise your ingenuity and skill in finding ways to organize and do the job faster, better, and cheaper. You have a budget and a mark to beat. After a few units, you can develop fast, smooth systems for accomplishing everything that has to be done, and swing a little more profit.

Plus no one is "looking over your shoulder;" they only worry about the quality after the job is finished.

A Couple of Cautions

If you have a whole series of units to clean and you do them all at once, in a row, you can make good time and hold expenses down. If, on the other hand, the client gives you five or ten units to do but three of them have to be done in a hurry, or they call you up suddenly to do one, it will kill you. Never forget that setup and travel time, and mileage cost for one unit or ten will be the same.

You'll lose money doing per-unit jobs piecemeal or hit and miss. You need to agree to and do them in bulk. Back and forth or "on call assignments" will cut your bottom line badly.

PER SQUARE FOOT PRICING

Per square foot sounds the simplest and would be, if all building and cleanup requirements were the same—which they aren't! I've seen this approach work well in:

1. Specific area cleaning (floors, carpets, etc.)
2. Tract residential projects

Specific Areas

Your square foot price should be regulated by how much is to be done, not only the nature and difficulty, but the size of the job. I charge 16¢ a square foot on the average to extract carpets, but if I had 3 football-field size casino carpets to do, I'd do them for 8¢ and do them well. For example:

If all the carpets are to be vacuumed and spotted (they are new)
3¢ a square foot

If all the carpets are to be extracted
10-16¢ a square foot

If all the hard floors are to be swept, spotted, and mopped
4¢ a square foot

If all the hard floors are to be stripped and given 2 coats of finish
16¢ a square foot

(For more examples, see the "Production Rates Table" on page 15.)

Beware of windows on square foot pricing—some are a snap, some incredibly complicated.

Residential or Tract Housing

A lot of our construction cleanup market is housing, and there may be 20, 40, 80, or even 200 units in a job. They vary a little in square footage, but are usually quite similar in construction and cleanup needs. You'll know from cleaning one or two on an hourly basis what it costs per square foot by dividing your final bill by the square footage of the house.

You have to learn your own square footage number for overall cleaning. I've heard "experts" quote from 5¢ to 25¢ per square foot.

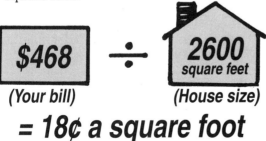

$468 (Your bill) ÷ **2600 square feet** (House size)

= 18¢ a square foot

PRICING BY BID

Pricing by bid (my favorite) is a combo of the last three pricing methods. It has the most of everything: risk, freedom, and profit potential, and is a good way to go once you get to know the work, the job, the season, and the general contractor involved.

Bidding is a simple matter of counting and measuring and multiplying—which is basic arithmetic.

Bidding is also a complex business of timing starts and finishes, juggling multiple jobs, and controlling how and when the craftspeople leave the site.

Always bid construction cleanup with options. That way, if the client adds or subtracts duties/work, you have flexibility to add or subtract (adjust) costs.

And get the client to sign the spec sheet, not just the price contract.

Here are a couple of construction cleanup bids you can use as a guideline, starting on page 16.

PRODUCTION RATES TABLE					
JOB / DESCRIPTION	SUPPLY FACTOR PER GROSS JOB COST	TOTAL COST PER EACH OR SQ. FT	DEGREE OF DIFFICULTY SQUARE FEET OR UNITS DONE PER HOUR		
			LIGHT	MEDIUM	HEAVY
CEILING CLEANING					
Smooth enamel (wash)	3%	COST PER SQUARE FT. →	.05	.06	.07
Textured enamel (wash)	3%		.06	.07	.08
Latex semi-tex (dry sponge)	3%		.03	.04	.05
Acoustic tile (dry sponge)	10%		.04	.05	.06
Acoustic tile (spray bleach)	20%		.15	.16	.18
Wood (finished)	3%		.05	.06	.07
"Cottage cheese"/fleck	-0-		GET A NEW ARCHITECT NEXT TIME		
WALL CLEANING					
Smooth enamel 10' or lower	3%	COST PER SQUARE FT. →	.04	.06	.07
Textured enamel 10' or lower	3%		.05	.07	.08
Enamel wall 10-15 ft	3%		.05	.07	.08
Wall covering–smooth	3%		.04	.06	.07
Wall covering–weave or fabric	4%		.10	.11	.12
Tile walls	2%		.04	.06	.07
Paneling	2%		.05	.06	.07
Painted masonry block	3%		.07	.08	.09
FURNITURE CLEAN & POLISH					
Piano (console)	4-6%	COST PER EACH →	5.00	8.00	10.00
Piano (grand)	4-6%		10.00	13.00	15.00
Refrigerator	4-6%		3.00	4.00	5.00
Average TV	4-6%		1.00	1.50	2.00
Dresser	4-6%		3.00	4.00	5.00
Wood-metal/washable chairs	4-6%		1.80	2.10	2.50
Office chairs	4-6%		4.00	5.00	6.00
Office desk	4-6%		6.00	7.00	8.00
Mattress	4-6%		3.00	3.50	4.50
CARPET VACUUMING					
Small vac unobstructed	2%		12,000	10,000	8,000
Small vac obstructed	2%		9,000	7,000	5,000
Space vac open area	2%		15,000	12,000	8,000
Exterior billy goat	2%		12,000	10,000	7,000
CARPET CLEANING					
Bonnet/spin pad	10%	.05	1,500	1,200	1,000
Dry powder method	30%	.20	600	400	200
Rotary/extraction	3%	.16	800	600	400
Steam extraction method	3%	.10	1,200	900	600
Automatic shampooer	3%	.08	3,000	2,000	1,000
LIGHT FIXTURES					
Egg crate grill	4' 4%	3.00	7	6	4
	8' 4%	6.00	6	4	3
Open tube type	4' 5%	2.00	12	10	8
	8' 5%	2.50	10	8	6
Swing lens	4' 5%	2.00	15	12	10
	8' 5%	2.50	12	10	8
WINDOWS					
Small pane (hand)	2%	access!	300	200	100
Small–open (squeegee)	2%	access!	600	400	200
Large–obstructed	2%	access is everything!	3,600	2,000	1,500
Large–open	2%		6,000	9,000	2,500
Tucker	8%	average	SUPERFAST!!		

SAMPLE BID: **Per Hour Pricing**

PO Box 1692
Pocatello ID 83204
208-232-8598

Who ←

When ←

Submission Date _____

Attention: Jon Marshall Developers, Inc.
1355 Apache, Pocatello ID 83204

What ←
Where ←
How ←

Subject: Construction cleanup bid for
Bannock Elementary School,
1100 Oak Street, Pocatello ID 83201

> We will provide all necessary labor, supervision,
> protective materials, and equipment to totally
> clean, per your directions, the entire interior and
> exterior of said building, at the contract hour rate of
> $14.20 per working hour on the job, which applies
> to all employees. We can have from 3 to 7 people
> at the job site to gear ourselves efficiently to what-
> ever your schedule is.

We appreciate the opportunity to submit this quote, which
comes with our reputation and guarantee of quick and
satisfactory job performance.

This bid is based upon the work being done after completion of construction and prior to occupancy.

Don Aslett

Don Aslett

*This is not a contract. If they
accept, you need to write
things up in more detail before you start the job.*

SAMPLE BID: **Per Unit Pricing**

PO Box 1692
Pocatello ID 83204
208-232-8598

Submission Date _____

Attention: Jon Marshall Developers, Inc.
1355 Apache, Pocatello ID 83204

Subject: Construction cleanup bid for
Portneuf Valley Condominimums
2324 Tyhee Road, Pocatello ID 83202

We have determined that if we can clean on an uninterrupted schedule, we can perform professional interior construction cleanup at this facility for the cost of $120 per unit, leaving all units clean, sanitized, and "ready to use." We understand there are 180 units in this facility.

We appreciate the opportunity to submit this quote, which comes with our reputation and guarantee of quick and satisfactory job performance.

This bid is based upon the work being done after completion of construction and prior to occupancy.

Don Aslett

Don Aslett

This is not a contract. If they accept, you need to write things up in more detail before you start the job.

SAMPLE BID: **Per Square Foot Pricing**

PO Box 1692
Pocatello ID 83204
208-232-8598

Submission Date _____

Attention: Jon Marshall Developers, Inc.
1355 Apache, Pocatello ID 83204

Subject: Construction cleanup bid for
Marsh Creek Press Warehouse,
132 West Halliday, Pocatello ID 83204

We would like to submit our price of <u>25¢ per square foot</u> to provide complete interior construction cleanup service to said building. This cost includes all labor, supplies, materials, equipment, travel, etc. This price is based on starting and finishing the job within a 3-day span, and will include the following: Removal of dust on all flat surfaces to a height of 12 feet. Removing debris, labels, etc. Cleaning and sealing concrete floors. Washing interior and exterior of all windows. Cleaning all light fixtures,

We appreciate the opportunity to submit this quote, which comes with our reputation and guarantee of quick and satisfactory job performance.

Bid offer expires in 30 days.

Don Aslett

This is not a contract. If they accept, you need to write things up in more detail before you start the job.

SAMPLE BID: **Per Bid Pricing**

PO Box 1692
Pocatello ID 83204
208-232-8598

Submission Date _____

Attention: Jon Marshall Developers, Inc.
1355 Apache, Pocatello ID 83204

Subject: Construction cleanup bid for
Marsh Creek Press Office Building,
311 South Fifth Avenue, Pocatello ID 83201

We have examined your entire 8,000 square foot new facility at 311 South Fifth Avenue and for a total cost of $640.00, propose to perform the needed construction cleanup as follows:
1. Remove all construction dust, debris, labels, etc.
2. Vacuum and spot clean all carpet
3. Clean and wax all floors
4. Clean and polish all fixtures
      1. in bathroom
      2. lighting fixtures
5. Clean and wash interior and exterior of all windows
6. Remove all trash from area

We appreciate the opportunity to submit this quote, which comes with our reputation and guarantee of quick and satisfactory job performance.

This bid is based upon the work being done after completion of construction and prior to occupancy.

This is not a contract. If they accept, you need to write things up in more detail before you start the job.

Don Aslett

The Four Biggest Mistakes of Bidding

Now let's take a look at the four biggest mistakes in bidding. Make even one of them (no matter how good an accountant or mathematician you may be) and you're dead.

1. Bidding too high. Not good for you or them. Overcharging robs them, spoils you, and throws off your future accuracy. It doesn't do anything for your reputation, either.

2. Bidding too low. You lose money, start lowering your standards, and begin to dislike and resent the job itself. Bidding too low will gradually, or even quickly, put you out of business.

3. Bidding too late. One of the biggest reasons for not getting work is bidding late. Even the most accurate and attractive LATE bids are at a tremendous disadvantage.

4. Bidding uninformed. Your bid might be on time, accurate, and fair to all concerned, but you don't know the whole scope of the job. So you find out: (when you're in the middle of it) that there was another room, floor, or wing of the structure. Most friction and financial stress in construction cleanup comes from "add-ons" that crop up later, because you didn't ask enough questions, or the client says, "How about throwing this in?"

Define and redefine "Broom Clean." Head off misunderstandings, disappointments, and hard feelings. Contractors, like restaurants, businesses, and homes, have different standards of "clean." What does "clean" mean to the person you are discussing a possible job with?

Always find out, and make clear: Who hauls off the big stuff (inside and out)? Do you have to make the place "ready to move into" clean or just roughly clean it after construction?

If you are bidding a job for the government, check with them to see if the Davis-Bacon act applies to it (www.dol.gov/compliance/laws/comp-dbra.htm). If so, be sure your bid includes adequate wages for this requirement.

Knowing and bidding accurately on all the work you do will not only produce a real profit for you, but will project leadership and confidence to your clients and employees. Estimating and submitting a clean and precise bid for the work you are to perform is a simple procedure that takes little time and lots of horse sense.

Remodeling Jobs

When it comes to the final details of the work there is little (if any) difference between construction cleanup on a remodeling job and a new building... UNLESS you get involved in the initial teardown. Remember when remodeling is done the old has to be ripped, torn, blasted, or chiseled out first, which means a lot of dust, grit, loose nails, piles of old plumbing and splintered wood, and possible damage to the good area. If a remodeled building is handed to you in good condition, it makes little difference in how you bid, or how you equip yourself, etc. But if you have to get involved in the phase of tearing out and hauling off the "old," it is another matter. Be wise as a serpent and tread like an angel on your bid and time commitment in this case, as you will need an expanded dimension of expertise and equipment.

PREPARING PROPOSALS AND PRESENTING THEM

The basic beginning of all construction cleanup jobs is when a client (after they track you down or you make a pitch) ends up asking you for a bid or price quotation. You then go through all the hoops of seeing the site, asking questions, looking, measuring, thinking, and figuring to come up with a price to do the job. And then comes the wait to see if you are rewarded—the contract, or "getting the go-ahead," as we call it. Let's look at several things here that do a lot to determine whether or not you are awarded a job or contract.

1. Your reputation/job history (a big factor), references.

2. How well and fast they think you can do the job.

3. The price you are offering (is it fair/competitive?).

4. How well you sell yourself and this particular job to them.

I can't help you too much right now with numbers one and two, but following my advice in this book will help you a lot with number three. And on number four, you can really help yourself with a professional, convincing proposal. Over and over, I've seen companies that were total failures on the first three items—a little on the shady side, slow, and way overbid—get the contract because of a great sales job in the proposal and presentation. And over and over and over again I've seen companies maybe like yours, who have wonderful reputations, can do the job bunny quick and right, and who bid perfectly competitively, even bid low, yet not get the job because of poor presentation. I wouldn't advise a phone call full of theory or a few jottings on a piece of paper handed to the superintendent to toss in his lunch pail and read later. These days, with the aid of a computer and a good-quality copier you can do a proposal package for pennies that will knock their socks off. Here are just a couple of solid steps to take and an illustration of what makes a good proposal (you can alter it to fit you, of course).

The Proposal

You visit the site, get all the measurements and figures, the time expectations, the tour, and often, in an hour or even less, if you're experienced you can come up with a price. I'd advise you not to hand it to the prospective client right then or tell them. Take it home, and type it up in detail, including all of the things you've talked about and been concerned about. Then outline all you are going to do—write it all out plain and clear and complete.

Now just by going a step or two further you can really enhance your chance of getting a job, and raise the builder's confidence in you. Include your bid price and outline sheet in a nice bound packet.

Spiral binding only costs a couple dollars and really makes a presentation look well put together. Many copy shop, FedEx or UPS stores, and office supply superstores will do spiral binding for you.

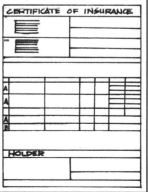

The cover looks great with your company name and logo. If you want to use color, this is the place for it. With the help of a computer/printer, you can add a line with the name and address of the company that your proposal has been prepared for.

The cover letter tells of your commitment to the work or project and thanks them for the opportunity to bid on it—this goes on your letterhead.

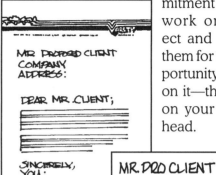

Next, include some **references**, something that shows your history and credentials—your credibility. Be impressive but brief.

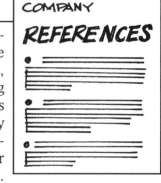

Next is your **certificate of insurance or bonding** or whatever (so they won't have to ask or beat it out of you). Your insurance company will be happy to make one for you. This gives a potential client confidence that your operation is in order, safe, honest, protected, etc., thus he or she is, too. See page 34 for the insurance you may need in construction cleanup.

Procedure page. This is optional, but I always do it now that I'm seasoned in the cleaning business. This is just a simple little outline or sketch of how you are going to do the job for them, what you will use, and when. By briefly telling them

the chemicals, cleaners, and procedures you intend to use, and who will be using them, you'll immediately take yourself out of the other bidders' league. (It doesn't hurt to toss in a little hint here of "look what I know that the other bidders might not know and ruin your Burmese burlap wall covering.") Don't you like it when your doctor, dentist, or mechanic takes the time to tell you what they intend to do before they begin? And isn't this a reason you choose some over others? Keep this to one page.

The Bid Sheet/price page (see sample next page)—always sign this. There is a place on this form for the customer's signature, and once he/she signs this, it becomes a contract.

Bid Sheet

Submitted to:	Idaho State University John O'Brien	Date:	8/25/___
		Attention:	Jerry/Richard
Street:	9301 Corbin Ave	Job Description:	Construction Cleanup
City, ST, Zip:	Pocatello ID 83204		Academic Buildings

1. Earl Pond Student Center—Construction Cleanup: New Restrooms 1st Floor

- Remove labels from new fixtures—sinks, stools, urinals (Men's Rooms)
- Remove caulk, putty, etc., from all fixtures
- Clean and sanitize fixtures
- Clean and polish dispensers
- Remove construction dust from ceilings, walls, partitions, doors, and all horizontal surfaces—use vacuum to capture all dust
- Dust windowsills and frames
- Wash windows interior/exterior—remove labels
- Vacuum floors using wet-dry/backpack vacuums
- Wet mop floor with sanitizing solution. Floor will be streak-free when dry

2. New Computer Room: Luke IT Laboratory

- Remove construction dust from ceilings, walls, partitions, doors, and all horizontal surfaces—use vacuum to capture dust
- Remove dust from light fixtures using backpack vacuum and dusting tool
- Dust windowsills and frames
- Wash windows interior/exterior—remove labels
- Vacuum carpets using vacuum with beater bar
- Remove any spots from carpet

3. Remove construction debris and cardboard from Luke IT Laboratory to compactor behind Food Technology building. Broom clean area after dumping.

Bid Amount: $1515.00

We propose to furnish labor and materials according to above specifications.
All material is guaranteed to be as specified. All work to be completed in a workmanlike manner according to standard practices. Any alteration or deviation from above specifications involving extra costs will be executed only upon written orders, and will be an extra charge over and above estimate. Company maintains full liability and Worker's Compensation insurance. Our employees are bonded.

Authorized Signature:_____

Note: This bid may be withdrawn by us if not accepted within ____60____ days.

Acceptance of proposal: The above prices, specifications and conditions are satisfactory and are hereby accepted. You are authorized to do the work as specified. Payment will be made as outlined above.

Date of Acceptance:_____   Signature:_____

The Presentation

You have some options here now with your wonderful, superb, brilliant piece of work.

1. You can let the mail carrier deliver it for you. Okay, but this will not have the impact of presenting it in person.

2. You can drop it off at the job site. Great, but chances are you won't get much in-person selling done and the proposal will have to carry itself. Also, the right person to deliver it to may not be there.

3. You can take it to the owner's office and ask for ten minutes to explain it and generally they will let you!

Number three is your best option. Go for it first, then resort to number two, and if all else fails, mail it (in an official-looking envelope, of course). Don't fax prices and bids—it's way too public and uncertain.

If you get an appointment to present your bid, take extra copies of the proposal with you and if you can, take the person who will be running the job with you. The reason you take extra proposals is that the owner might have a supervisor there or want to give a copy to the supervisor or an assistant or someone else who is sitting in the room. You can always take the extras back. I like extra copies; they can be used on the job, and as a format model for other presentations. It also doesn't hurt to have a couple of backup copies in the file.

Don't hand them the proposal right away—sit down and discuss it, quickly page through the letter, certificate, etc., and then hand them the copies. If you hand them the proposal right off, they will ignore all your references and sales stuff and go right to the price page. Make your visit short and leave, again assuring them of your quality, commitment, horsepower, etc.

Once you get a proposal that works, doing one for the next such job is only a process of inserting the price sheet and client address, because you have a "boilerplate" example. After you have worked for a certain company for a number of jobs, or years, a formal office presentation or visit might not be needed, but the whole nice "booklet" approach to the proposal is, so keep it up.

PO Box 1692
Pocatello ID 83204
208-232-8598

Date goes here

Construction cleanup for Sawtooth Valley Apartments,
104 Buckskin Road, Inkom, ID 83245

_____
Total $8608.00

Thank you,

signature

Too Brief

How to Bill Out a Construction Cleanup Job

Construction cleanup, regardless of how you price it (bid, by the hour, or square feet) always has some variables and seldom ends up exactly at the agreed-upon price. The key to keeping everyone happy is to bill out NOW, just as soon as the job is finished or after an agreed-upon section of the job is done. Always itemize and explain.

PO Box 1692
Pocatello ID 83204
208-232-8598

Date goes here

Construction cleanup for Sawtooth Valley Apartments,
104 Buckskin Road, Inkom, ID 83245

Jan. 27—Feb. 26, 20___
Cleaning interior of all 104 apartments as per schedule
and specifications agreed upon (attached)
.... @$72.00......... $7,488.00

Policing interior driveway in Standish complex
....$160.00

Extracting carpet as requested in units #24, 82,
46, and 21, total of 6000 sq. ft. @ $.16
....$960.00

Removal of extra load of debris, redo of 3 units after phone
installation
.... —no charge

_____
Total $8608.00

Thank you,
 signature goes here

Bonus the Bill!

All agreed-upon work (as well as added on or request work) should be itemized and billed. If it is documented, the charges are fair, and the work satisfactory, you will usually be paid without dispute.

There are times, however, when you should offer a little extra—free. Everyone loves to think (or know) that they got their money's worth, or a good deal or something extra. I've found there are lots of little petty or even disputable jobs that crop up in the course of a job. It's unclear who should do them and who should pay for them and maybe all of them together only took you five hours, $70 actual cost to you. Detailing, explaining and billing them—even though it is only fair that you be paid for them—is often an irritant to the boss/owner. Often it's better to bill for the unquestionably billable stuff and then add on a detailed list of the extra piddly things you did willingly and write "NO CHARGE" by those items.

Trust me, this will be a little thank-you, a gesture of goodwill they won't forget and it is probably the cheapest marketing expenditure for future jobs you'll ever do.

Example:

TO: Mr. Cartright, owner

We complied with a number (30) of last-minute requests, orders, and demands by "everyone" on this job. These included: vacuumed newly arrived furniture, shampooed office 33 (for the third time), drove a renter to the airport, pressure-washed the patio after a storm, recleaned the cafeteria floor after vendor, captured three bats and two cats that got into the building, removed signs and cleaned up construction tape inside, etc. ....All at NO CHARGE to you.

Thank you for the work and cooperation. We appreciate being treated well by you folks and the subcontractors.

Don Aslett, crew leader
Varsity Contractors, Inc.

THINGS LIKE THIS ARE A GOOD INVESTMENT!

Some Cash-Flow Cautions

Money is always a delicate subject, even when it's been earned and the client is not short of cash. Sloppy handling of things here can cause payment delays and hurt a good business relationship. So, do all you can from the start to prevent this.

1. Check out who you will be working for and know who will be paying you. Find out if they really pay their bills! The end of the year or job usually means the end of the money and tolerance and too often "cleaners" are at the end of the pay list.

2. Before you begin a job, write out perfectly clearly what you'll do, where, how, when, and for how much.

3. Make sure that when you will be paid is clear. At the end of the job or in 30 or 60 days? At progress points?

4. Make sure every job is finished well and that all details are wrapped up so there is absolutely no callback.

5. Bill immediately upon completion, and make sure the bill is well detailed and makes it clear when the money is due.

6. If slow or no payment results, a friendly call or visit works better than a "demand dunner" letter. Make sure you are visiting the real controller of funds when you do this. They will know whether the money is available or not.

7. Quietly arrange and know the channel of lien capacity—when, who and how you, as a contractor, can lien the properties involved if you don't get paid. Then if it looks bleak, you can get an attorney and put a lien on the property. If done right, a lien will tie up the property until you are paid.

RECORDS/ DOCUMENTATION

I can't say enough about this and not to "prove" something or "get" anybody, but for good, smooth operation and organization at every stage of a construction cleanup job! Good records save arbitration, plus you'll get PAID FASTER!

You need records at every stage.

BEFORE: Doing a little paperwork here is THE key to construction cleanup—it can make or break you and the job. No matter how badly you need or want the work, or how tempting it might be, you need to find out and know all the whats, whys, wheres, whens, and hows involved before you proceed. We have a tendency to let circumstances and desperation decide the price and product and if we guess wrong, no one comes out ahead. On pages 8-10 is an objective checklist you should run through before taking on any job.

DURING: No matter how careful a bid or estimate you did, there will be surprises (good and bad) here—including injustices, abuses, overruns, theft, and help problems. Especially if you have several crews working, make sure their daily hours and attendance records are kept up. It's especially expensive if you collect bits of paper in a pile and try to figure it all out later. You will not only be sorry, but inaccurate on billing and bottom line. Keep a central log (history/journal) of every job.

AFTER: Do a summary and analysis, add up columns, check records: what was cleaned, how fast, for how much. Do an accurate "job sheet" (see page 60) so you know exactly what it all cost and how much profit was made.

True professionals know... what their services are worth and exactly how to price them.

ME—

THE BIG BROKER OF CONSTRUCTION CLEANUP

There are, in the business climate today, tens of thousands of people who have gotten the idea reading "success" magazines that the way to make it in this world is to be the big wheel—the broker. The broker gets jobs and then finds someone else, or other companies to do them while he takes a percentage or a commission. The idea is to get twenty jobs going and have someone else earn your living while you just walk around with a clipboard, and a cell phone. This seldom works in the cleaning end of things, especially in construction cleanup where the resident/owner is there watching and worrying about all the little things. If you are thinking about "subcontracting" out your job—be careful! Mighty careful.

A technique often tried is bidding the job and then getting another member of our trade to bid the same job for us lower and then let them do

it and we take the profit difference. When done right, this can be a sound, ethical business practice—lots of businesses do this with their smaller jobs. But it isn't a good idea in construction cleanup. Contract nothing (and that includes maid service) to any who aren't really subcontractors. Contracting out unit price work to employees or even groups that are not functioning independently and legally as bona fide contractors, is illegal. You can also be sued for default on their part or accidents they are involved in. Since they don't have official legal status as a bona fide contractor, you are liable.

Until you are big, rich, famous, seasoned and loved by all contractors, I sure wouldn't advise giving your work to someone else. Besides, if you are smart, efficient, and capable, why would you want to give your work away for a tiny percentage?

Some Construction Cleanup Pitfalls to Be Prepared for

● In 5 out of 5 new buildings, a number of disputes and problems develop and accelerate during and around the final completion and cleanup. Generally all trades are behind and in a hurry. Tempers and patience are thin, bosses and demands multiply, and you can expect blame that you don't deserve!

● 4 out of 5 new buildings have a delayed opening (aren't on schedule), generally because of slow finalization and finish-up of the construction itself. This erratic schedule will pass on to you and you'll get last-minute, emergency assignments.

● You can also expect a multi-boss attack. The builder, the owner, the decorators, and some of the subcontractors and movers will all be giving you orders and demands.

● Redo is a fact of life in construction cleanup. All kinds of people somehow will come behind your perfectly cleaned area and trash it. So cleanup has to be done again and then who pays?

● A tendency for the "cleaners" to get left out of the payment line is common, or the general contractor is out of money by the time he gets to you.

● Severe cold/hot weather will slow the speed of construction cleanup and add some risks to it.

Remember these six pitfalls and be prepared for them, so you can have a pleasant, profitable cleaning job.

YOUR SET-UP CHECKLIST

The "smart before you start" approach to any job.

The Schedule:
- ☐ When will the job start?
- ☐ When will it end?
- ☐ When will the site be available? (If you don't have a firm answer, **don't start**. Trying to clean while the construction crew is still in the area is taking two steps forward and one step back.)
- ☐ Will you or your crew need training before you start?

Authority:
- ☐ Has the boss or authority on this job been identified? Who is your contact on the job?

Keys:
- ☐ Do you have access not only to the buildings or units themselves, but also to closets, alarm gates, and parking?
- ☐ Will you need a security pass? Do you have it?

Utilities:
- ☐ Is water available? Hot?
- ☐ Will there be an electricity source?
- ☐ Where do you dispose of your trash?
- ☐ Will restrooms be available?

Care Labels:
- ☐ Ask the contractor to provide cleaning and care instructions, tags, and warranties, for all fixtures, counters, and surfaces, if they are special or new, until you become familiar with them.

Findability:
- ☐ Get a typed directory of management and crews of all tradespeople and subcontractors in the building, with phone numbers, so there will be no excuse for communication barriers.

WHO'S THE BOSS HERE?

Let me say a little more now about the "Authority" mentioned on the checklist. Ultimately the person(s) who is paying is the big boss of operations, however, the builder/contractor (not the owner) generally has charge of the actual construction cleanup. We (you and me, the cleaners) answer to the boss or head of the building crew, usually the foreman. This is an important point of organization—be sure you know (for sure) who sets the rules and rewards. During the home stretch of finishing a job or building, everyone is anxious to get their "two cents in" and advise about where, when, what, and how things are cleaned. You must answer to one person, through one channel—be sure to establish this and then honor it. It will mean job security and less stress for both parties.

WHAT ABOUT INSURANCE?

Think about this. You are left, generally alone, in charge of, in control of, and responsible for, what may be a multimillion-dollar structure. You are armed with powerful machines, razors, acids, and solvents, and may have some "inepts" working for you. You are insured for liability, not stupidity, so if you ruin something while cleaning it, you pay for it.

Speaking of insurance—most smart contractors will require you to carry a minimum of one million dollars of insurance. They will want you to carry liability and full Worker's Compensation for your employees.

There are two aspects to consider here:

1. Risk of what you might inflict on them or their facility.
2. Risk of what they might inflict on you.

Our different states have different insurance requirements for contractors (such as liability, Worker's Comp, general damage coverage). Some contractors, if they like or trust you, might even include you under their umbrella policy. Insurance is not a difficult item to deal with, all you need to do is:

1. Ask local contractors/builders what the requirements are.
2. Review your current coverage for compatibility.
3. Call an insurance broker and ask—there are plenty of them around and they have tables/ rates to instantly cover you for anything you need to be covered for.

KEEP THE CERTIFICATE OF INSURANCE ON FILE AND ACCESSIBLE ALWAYS.

Safe? Sorry? **Sued!**

SAFETY IS SERIOUS BUSINESS

Safety precautions are not something you take just to "get you by" or "to get the job."

Any accident that happens on a job (breaking a finger, a neck, or someone's new equipment), or any injury to you, your coworkers, or client, will instantly:

1. Upset and distract you and others

2. Cause pain and possibly disability or worse

3. Take your time

4. Consume your resources (people and property)

5. Wipe out the profit of the job

6. Lose you confidence, prestige, and future jobs

7. Raise your future insurance rates

SAFETY CHECKLIST

☐ All of your equipment (including electric cords) is in good working order.

☐ You carry insurance and Worker's Compensation coverage.

☐ You and your workers have all the safety clothing and equipment you need.

☐ Vehicles are parked out of harm's way.

☐ You are aware of any unfinished electrical work.

Rose Galera of Hawaii has one of the best lists of safety rules I've seen (see the following page)—yours should be similar. Adjust this or add to it to fit your situation, then have all of your employees sign and follow it!

Sample Safety Policy:

Notice of General Safety Rules

The following is a list of the minimum safety requirements for this construction project. This list is a supplement to the safety program available at the project office. Each worker must be aware of and comply with these requirements. Failure to comply will be cause for immediate dismissal.

1. Hard hats will be worn at all times, in all construction areas.

2. Minimum clothing protection will be full length pants and T-shirts.

3. Hard-soled leather work shoes or boots are required.

4. Eye protection, ear protection, respiratory protection and gloves are required, depending on your work assignments. (These will be furnished.)

5. Glass beverage containers are not permitted.

6. Alcoholic beverages and drugs are prohibited.

7. Firearms are prohibited.

8. Dispose of trash in designated receptacles only.

9. Horseplay or roughhousing is not permitted.

10. Personal vehicles will be parked out of construction areas and as directed by your supervisor.

11. Follow all warnings on package labels. Your supervisor is required by law to instruct you about handling materials that are hazardous to your health.

12. The "common cup" for drinking water is not permitted.

13. Sanitary facilities are provided on the job site. Do not use any other area.

14. Report unsafe equipment, hazardous conditions, and unsafe acts to your supervisor.

15. Report all accidents to your supervisor immediately.

Your cooperation in maintaining a safe, accident-free job site is appreciated.

I understand the above regulations and agree to comply with these and any other safety rules on this project. I also understand that I may be dismissed from this project if I fail to comply.

Signature_____

Thanks to Rose Galera, Clean Plus Systems, Pearl City, Hawaii!

HOW TO ORGANIZE YOUR CONSTRUCTION CLEANUP

The owner of the cleaning company will have the responsibility of outlining, scheduling, and running the cleanup program. If you're the supervisor, someone else will handle the details, if of course they are experienced and competent. On pages 40-42 are two forms that will help you identify, prepare for, and keep track of all the "to-do's" on a construction cleanup job. The Work Schedule on pages 40-41 can also be included in a bid.

Hire people that can specialize on the job. Some are good window washers, others good floor mechanics, etc. Use them in the capacities they are best suited for. The job will be short, so don't be concerned about employees' boredom with only having one repetitive task. Instead use it to your advantage. Arrive at a fair rate for the work which is somewhat higher than regular cleanup duties and offer this alternative. Usually the work will be done faster and more happily.

Staggered, Specialized Cleaning

On a large job, a good procedure is to do staggered, specialized cleaning. For instance, one crew will clean bathrooms only, followed by wall washers and dusters, followed by vacuumers, followed by detailers. Usually a leader is necessary in a situation like this. It is important to keep your job supervisor abreast of your progress and any difficulties. Cleaning supervisors are usually working every day and need constant awareness to operate effectively. It is also important on these jobs to have your work checked off by the client after completion. Do this by sections, rooms, duties, or areas (the area could be dirty again in hours).

If a job is big and long and includes lots of units, I set up crews on a strict production method of specialized cleaning. This system gives us speed along with efficiency. The following is a list of the possible different positions on a residential crew.

- The pre-bathroom person guts it out—does the rough cleanup, removes labels, trash, etc.

- Second to go to the room is the bathroom crew. This is broken down into two-person teams: one does the tub, the other does everything else except the floors.

- Maids—they dust fixtures, polish chrome, and polish the woodwork.

- The pre-vacuum person picks up all large pieces of debris, and finishes by mopping the bathroom floors.

- Interior window people wash windows, and clean window frames and air conditioning units.

- The suite mirror person does mirrors other than bathroom mirrors.

- The vacuum people usually work as a team—one does open areas, the other detail vacuuming. When they are done, the interior of the room is finished and signed off by a supervisor. This again is an important step, because often, at least one third of the rooms will be gone back into by various trades and they will mess them up. With backup reports, you will be paid to reclean these rooms. Without them, you will clean them again for nothing.

- Last person in the room is the outer door and door frame person. The frames may have not just dust, but paint and glue to be removed. This is a time consumer.

- Hallways and stairwells are done last. Vacuum, wipe down walls, dust hand rails, etc.

If the job is small, one person can do all of these things alone or with one helper.

A BASIC FLOW CHART to assist you with your timing decisions

1. Determine the extent of construction cleanup needed.

   a. It will take _____ (days, weeks, months)

   b. It will cost _____

   c. The approximate finish time _____

2. Sixty days before you need them, select competent crews or groups to do the work.

3. Tour the construction cleanup site or facility with the site boss 30 days before any anticipated work. (Always tour, don't bid by plans.)

4. Request a plan of attack, including size of crew and working schedule, in writing from the contractor or the site supervisor.

5. Physically check all your equipment and supplies and have them ready in the area 10 days before starting.

6. Follow the progress of the building project and get an accurate commitment date from the areas of building slated to be finished first. At this time, note any late shipments, strikes, or anything else that could affect the time of completion. Relay this in writing to the contractor, including the furniture move-in schedule. Furniture moving is something you might get to do and they need to know you can (for an extra charge of course).

7. Make sure you have a list and outline of exactly what the client wants you to do. "Just clean it up" isn't good enough.

   The original proposal, if it was outlined properly, can be your best tool to use as the outline for the job. For example, ask contractors to submit a detailed ***Exactly What I Will Do*** sheet and use it for the outline of duties in the proposal, and then on the actual job. This shows control and professionalism and helps you get the job!

8. Don't start any work singly that can be done in a group or crew, especially if it might have to sit for any length of time before the rest of the work is completed. Doing work in one big steady application is better than in dozens of small sporadic ones.

9. See page 56 for how to handle redos, the curse of construction cleanup.

VARSITY CONTRACTORS, INC.
Construction Cleanup
WORK SCHEDULE

Project: _____

Location: _____

AREA

ITEMS / SUGGESTED SPECIFICS	OFFICE/ADMIN	SUITE	DATA PROCESSING	KITCHEN	LOBBIES/HALLS	CAFETERIA	LOUNGES	RESTROOM/BATH	STAIRWAYS	ELEVATORS	HVAC	STORAGE	GARAGE/DOCKS	JANITOR CLOSET
FLOORS														
Remove trash & debris														
Sweep or dust														
Damp mop/disinfect restrooms														
Remove black marks/stains														
Scrub														
Scrub & finish/seal														
Remove oil deposits or spills														
Hose/wash down														
Remove dust, glue from baseboards														
CARPETS														
Detail vacuum														
Spot clean														
Shampoo (extract)														
Bonnet clean														
Antistatic treatment														
Soil retardant														
DUST														
Dust racks/shelves														
Dust all flat surfaces														
Dust fixtures/hangings														
High dust														
FURNITURE														
Dust														
Clean/polish														
Unpack/assemble														
Transport to rooms														
Remove labels														
FIXTURES														
Clean & polish mirrors														
Clean/polish chrome/stainless														
Remove labels														
Clean & sanitize tubs, sinks, showers, toilets, urinals														
Clean/polish vanity & cupboards														
Clean countertops														
WALLS/DOORS/PARTITIONS														
Dust														
Spot clean walls														
Wash walls														
Polish wood panels														
Clean/vacuum wall coverings														
Wash & polish doors, door jambs														
Remove glue & debris														

Page 2

Construction Cleanup
WORK SCHEDULE

	OFFICE/ADMIN	SUITE	DATA PROCESSING	KITCHEN	LOBBIES/HALLS	CAFETERIA	LOUNGES	RESTROOM/BATH	STAIRWAYS	ELEVATORS	HVAC	STORAGE	GARAGE/DOCKS	JANITOR CLOSET
CEILINGS														
Clean ceiling sprinkler heads														
Clean debris from light fixtures														
Clean ceiling vents														
GLASS														
Wash door glass														
Wash display windows														
Wash interior windows & frames														
Wash exterior windows & frames														
Wash partition windows														
Wash mirrors														
EXTERIOR														
Pick up trash & debris														
Remove trash & debris from premises														
Sweep parking lot														
Sweep sidewalks														
SUPPLIES														
Buffers, vacuums														
Cleaning equipment														
Cleaning supplies & chemicals														
Seal/finish														
Cleaning cloths/mops														
Swing stage														
Cable climber														

VARSITY CONTRACTORS, INC., COST SCHEDULE

1. Cleaning services per WORK SCHEDULE $ _____
   Area or rooms excluded _____
   _____

2. DETAIL PRICING

   | $ _____ per sq. ft. ☐
   a. Carpet   ☐ vacuum   ☐ spot clean   ☐ shampoo $ _____ per cleaning ☐

   b. Tile floor   ☐ sweep   ☐ wet mop   ☐ scrub $ _____ per sq. ft. ☐
                ☐ scrub & finish (# coats ____) $ ____ per cleaning ☐

   c. Bath/restrooms # _____   ☐ seal floor
                                    ☐ clean & polish fixtures
                                    ☐ wash walls/partitions $ _____ per cleaning

   d. Windows & frames   ☐ interior $ _____ per cleaning
                          ☐ exterior $ _____ per cleaning
   e. Other _____ $ _____ per cleaning
            _____ $ _____ per cleaning

3. ADDITIONAL CHARGES
   For all hours over and above the foregoing due to unforeseen conditions,
   or additional requests after agreed-upon cleaning is completed. $ _____ per hour

VARSITY CONTRACTORS, INC.

Construction Cleanup
To Do List

NAME: _____

DATE: _____

JOB NAME: _____ JOB #: _____ ADDRESS: _____

THINGS TO DO: TOOLS: SUPPLIES:

1.☐ _____ _____ _____
2.☐ _____ _____ _____
3.☐ _____ _____ _____
4.☐ _____ _____ _____
5.☐ _____ _____ _____
6.☐ _____ _____ _____
7.☐ _____ _____ _____
8.☐ _____ _____ _____
NOTES: _____ _____ _____
_____ _____ _____
_____ _____ _____

JOB NAME: _____ JOB #: _____ ADDRESS: _____

THINGS TO DO: TOOLS: SUPPLIES:

1.☐ _____ _____ _____
2.☐ _____ _____ _____
3.☐ _____ _____ _____
4.☐ _____ _____ _____
5.☐ _____ _____ _____
6.☐ _____ _____ _____
7.☐ _____ _____ _____
8.☐ _____ _____ _____
NOTES: _____ _____ _____
_____ _____ _____
_____ _____ _____

JOB NAME: _____ JOB #: _____ ADDRESS: _____

THINGS TO DO: TOOLS: SUPPLIES:

1.☐ _____ _____ _____
2.☐ _____ _____ _____
3.☐ _____ _____ _____
4.☐ _____ _____ _____
5.☐ _____ _____ _____
6.☐ _____ _____ _____
7.☐ _____ _____ _____
8.☐ _____ _____ _____
NOTES: _____ _____ _____
_____ _____ _____
_____ _____ _____

OTHER: 1.☐ _____   3.☐ _____
            2.☐ _____   4.☐ _____

TIMING

The actual physical work of the cleaning itself is the easy part of a construction cleanup job. Setup, timing, and coordination are the critical parts. "Overlap" is the 7-letter word you don't want to hear. Even though you can't control the 10+ trades that will come before you (glazier, tiler, carpet layer, roofer, framer, plumber, electrician, phone installer, mover, painter) you have to work behind them and as mentioned earlier, you only want to do this once.

It's really tough to begin or do construction cleanup until everyone (all the other trades) are finished and OUT. You need to exercise careful control over this, as most of the time you'll be called to start while the last subs are finishing (project finish-up is a panic generally). Most foremen don't realize this and will launch you prematurely. So you must assess, find out the status before you show up with your crew and equipment. Then, confidently and professionally, inform the boss of the situation (that there is a crowd there, or carpets aren't down, etc.), that you are ready and willing to go and will get in to clean the minute the coast is clear. If you calmly make this clear, all will usually be well after that. If the boss says START ANYWAY, you better do it and keep good records.

Any time you are working with a gang of others around, it is slower (because of distractions). And there is lots of redoing and equipment borrowing. Worst of all, subs seeing you there have a tendency to leave their mess for you.

However, starting too late can be just as costly in money and time lost. Trying to clean the same windows after landscaping has been finished, or plush drapes have been hung, will give you bad, expensive results.

Once you have started, you will be under pressure to finish quickly since you are usually the last contractor working before the building can bring in any revenue for the owners. The best approach is to hold off the entire course of your cleanup work as long as possible, until everyone else is out, then use a competent crew and move quickly. It is most efficient, for example, to do inside and outside windows at the same time. Get the job done fast, in a few days—signed off and out!

When Is the Best Time to Do Your Work, Now?

Saturdays and holidays are super construction cleanup days!

Daylight is best for many reasons:

1. You can see clearly
2. Others can see you there, on the job
3. More security
4. Safer
5. Stores are open for emergency needs
6. You can find your help more easily and control them better

When you can, AVOID:

1. Extremely cold weather—products freeze, windows ice up, roads are bad, people are late, and numb hands do poor work
2. Very hot weather—windows dry too fast, and people are slow and draggy and inefficient
3. Working alone—two or more people is best for safety, security, lifting, holding, moving, etc.!

Phase Cleaning

As I've said, it's always best in construction cleanup to wait till all trades have finished, then enter with your crew and clean and then turn the key over to the owner—that's ideal and it is possible a lot of the time.

But the size and condition of a job can sometimes force your organization and schedule into a "phase" or section type cleaning. This means that sometimes, while the scaffolding is still up, or before anything has been moved onto or installed on the floor, they will want the ceiling or floors dusted or cleaned. This is called first or "initial pass through," "rough," or preliminary cleaning, and if it's requested, it's necessary, YOU DO IT!

Or you may sometimes have to break your cleaning into stages such as "Rough Cleaning," "Final Cleaning," and "Touch-Up Cleaning."

As I'll repeat over and over in this book, keep records, good records, keep your clients' requests recorded and on file and know their desires and reasoning so you can do what they want, when they want it. Do it so that you get credit for it—and paid for it. REDOs, or recleaning (which means they have to pay you twice for the same area) is the most volatile issue going. Keep good records so you can keep things clear, low-key, and well justified—for some reason at pay time they only remember the final and not the phase work!

On-site organization

All structures, domestic or commercial, have their general, common, familiar requirements, but just about all also have a few new, unique needs. Therefore, standard directions cannot be used. Every job should have a "tailored list" of duties and needs spelled out for the crew and contractors. This eliminates any misunderstandings and also serves as a checklist for the job. Here is a nice example used by Rose Galera from Clean Plus Systems in Hawaii for the various stages of an apartment construction cleanup job.

The first trip shall be rough cleaning and shall include but not be limited to the following.

Rough Cleaning

Date of cleaning: _____

Supervisor: _____ Building #: _____ Unit #: _____

Cleaners: _____

Work to be done

1. Remove any and all trash, dirt, and debris from the interior of the unit and dispose of as directed by the Contractor's Superintendent.

2. Clean all tubs, toilets, lavatories, kitchen sinks and appliances. Remove any and all temporary protection and labels not required to remain.

3. Clean out all kitchen cabinets and vanity cabinets. Clean all kitchen countertops and vanity tops.

4. Scrape and wash the inside and outside surfaces of all windows and sliding glass doors. Do not scrape windows or scratch frames.

5. Clean all windows and sliding glass door frames, sills, and tracks. Vacuum tracks as required. (Pay special attention to windows and tracks above stairways.)

6. Clean all utility closets, furnace closets, storage areas, garages, etc.

7. Clean all water heaters.

8. Clean water valve box (washing machine/dryer area)

The second trip shall be a final cleaning in preparation for the initial inspection by the Owner, such that the Owner could, if he so desired, take possession of, and occupy the unit upon completion of this initial inspection.

Final Cleaning

Date of cleaning: _____

Supervisor: _____ Building #: _____ Unit #: _____

Cleaners: _____

Prepare Unit for Final Inspection

1. Remove any and all trash, dirt, and debris from the interior of the unit and dispose of as directed by the Contractor's Superintendent.

2. Clean and polish kitchen cabinets, kitchen countertops, and vanity tops. Vacuum the inside of all cabinets, as required to remove dirt and debris. Polish all cabinets, vanities, and other stained woodwork and all stainless steel sinks using lemon oil or other polish.

3. Clean and shine the inside and outside surfaces of all windows and sliding glass doors.

4. Clean and shine all plumbing fixtures and related trim to a sanitary condition. Clean and shine all medicine cabinets, mirrors, and bath accessories.

5. Clean and shine all electrical fixtures and trim.

6. Clean and shine all appliances. Remove all packing materials, temporary labels, and operating and maintenance manuals. Place in kitchen drawers as directed.

7. Clean all wood base, casing, and sills. Clean all wood shelving.

8. Clean the outside and inside of all exterior doors, including the threshold. Clean and shine all interior doors.

9. Clean and shine all finish hardware.

10. Sweep and mop all VCT tile floors. Damp mop all tiles using a shine and conditioner in the mop water.

11. Sweep all exterior storage areas, garages, patios, and stoops.

12. Dust or vacuum walls as needed.

The third trip shall be a touch-up cleaning as required by the Contractor's Superintendent. It shall include but not be limited to the following.

Touch-Up Cleaning

Date of cleaning: _____

Supervisor:_____ Building #: _____ Unit #: _____

Cleaners: _____

Prepare unit for owner acceptance and occupant move in.

1. Check each unit. Clean, shine, dust, and/or vacuum as required to provide a "salable" unit.

2. Touch up and reshine, polish all cabinets, vanities, and other stained woodwork and all stainless steel sinks using lemon oil or other polish as approved by the Contractor's Superintendent.

   Additional trips or recleaning, if required in order to "sell" the unit, shall be performed as and when required by the Contractor's Superintendent.

   THIS SUBCONTRACTOR UNDERSTANDS THAT A COMPLETE PROFESSIONAL FINAL CLEANING JOB IS INTENDED.

Additional Cleaning

1.

2.

3.

4.

"You Are Here": Mapmaking

Construction cleanup is exciting, but an excitement we don't want here is that of getting or being lost—workers unable to locate each other or their equipment. There is generally enough confusion on a construction cleanup job without us adding to it. We also don't want our help spending an hour a day just "hunting."

After a week or so, we do finally learn all the names, members, and routes, but we can look like bumblers and lose image and money during that first week while we're learning.

If a job even approaches complex, get a floor plan or site layout and mark the areas you will be concerned with, by name and number and include any other appropriate information. Draw up your own map or layout if you have to. Make some copies and distribute them and post one in a central place. It's amazing how this will uncomplicate communication and how professional you'll look.

Remember: Just make up your own if outlines or sketches aren't already available.

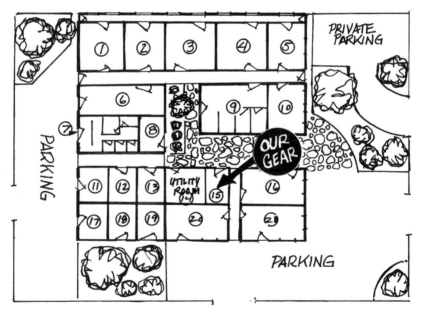

OFFICE BUILDING
COMPLEX

CONSTRUCTION CLEANUP WORK ETHICS AND RULES

Now, a little preamble before you amble through a construction cleanup job. Aside from cleaning skill, there are qualities like honesty, trust, loyalty, courtesy, and punctuality that affect how you will be seen by the many subs you have to work with, as well as the owners. So, always bow to the boundaries, keep the commandments of good construction relationships. Here they are, written up so they can be passed out or posted for any employees you may have.

1. Remember you are on, in, and around other people's properties during every job, which calls for a "visitor" level of respect.

2. Your opinions, appraisals, and criticisms of the place or people should be kept to yourself. You may relay them to your boss and no one else.

3. Radios, tape or CD players, cellular phones, and pagers or other personal gear are not allowed on the job.

4. Personal vehicles will be parked out away from construction sites so as not to interfere with the job traffic.

5. Without permission, don't tour friends or strangers through the facilities.

6. Respond immediately and positively to all client requests and complaints. Contact your supervisor if necessary.

7. Absolutely no abusive language (swearing and yelling) on the job. Horseplay, fighting, or other disruptive activities on the job site are also prohibited.

8. You are responsible for the condition, care, and safety of any client equipment you use. When you're done with it, leave it clean and stored properly in the designated place.

9. Wear a uniform and proper identification at all times.

10. Never loan or allow issued keys to a facility to get out of your hands.

Construction Cleanup:

A TIME TO PULL OUT YOUR PR SKILLS

Construction cleanup time is generally high tension time. The project is close to conclusion and all the contractors and subcontractors are tired of it and want to get *out* and paid right now. The owners and clients are tired of it all, too, and they want to get *in* right now. There is more irritation, blaming, excuses, and confusion than any other time in the course of the project. The telephone systems are being debugged, messing up walls, the poorly aimed sprinkler system is spotting the windows, etc. The more sensitive you are to this (and prepared to fix it), the more successful, profitable, and enjoyable your job will be. How fast and well the construction cleanup goes is one of the BIG factors in satisfying everyone.

Blessed Are the Peacemakers (for They Shall Be the Best Construction Cleaners)

There can be from 5 to 25 different trades and subcontractors on one construction job (carpenters, plumbers, roofers, cable TV people, landscapers, electricians, glaziers, flooring installers, phone installers, painters, tapers, masons, etc.) and you are one of them—the person who comes behind them all and makes all of their workmanship look good. If they all LIKE and RESPECT you, it can cut your workload 30%. Stay out of other subcontractors' squabbles, mind your own business—and you'll be much better off. MAKE NO ENEMIES ON THE JOB—even if someone borrows your best vacuum without asking (and ends up plugging it up). Love and work even with those who use you or your gear unkindly. Follow all the advice in this book about being professional, marking and storing tools (see page 62), making schedules, etc. All of these disciplines, if followed faithfully, will help make friends and eliminate situations that breed enemies. Out of ALL cleaning jobs this one needs your best manners.

Remember, if people don't like you, you can't clean well enough to please them.

1. Don't talk in terms of "your job" or "my job," use "us" and "we."

2. When you need to report on problems or shortcomings in a facility, combine your lacks with theirs on a general list rather than a "hang 'em," single-them-out list.

3. Don't say "the painters" or "the plumber." These people have names—use them.

4. Always try to work problems out with the tradespeople involved, before you take anything to the foreman.

5. POST your schedule and list of job duties, etc., publicly so the other trades can see it. This will set a standard and some boundaries and MOST fellow workers will honor that.

6. Sometimes when others "steal" your equipment they are actually doing your work for you. So don't come unglued when you find them removing their glue with your gear. This is why it's not a bad idea to bring some old equipment to construction jobs and have a little extra cleaning gear around.

7. Don't join in or side with people or groups that are forever murmuring, criticizing, and taking antagonistic stands. Be quiet and clean well and fast.

8. Don't flirt, join dirty joke clubs, or drink with "the gang." Cleaners don't do themselves any good here.

Don't Whine

Whatever you do, DON'T WHINE, complain, or criticize the other tradespeople, even if they are careless slobs. They can really punish the place if they are irritated at you. Do ALL you can to get them to help you, like:

1. Provide a few extra tools or containers, so they have the means to clean up after themselves.

2. Close off the areas that have been "final cleaned" with caution tape and a warning/friendly reminder that lets them know your job is done here and **they** will be responsible for any further cleanup necessary, not you.

Keep It All Confidential

As soon as you start bidding work, all kinds of ethics come into play. Being honest, fair, reliable, on time, etc., is part of the bid, even of getting it. You might see, hear, or otherwise find out about details of costs and politics and gossip or whatever in the course of bidding, and all of this you must keep to yourself and your bid. When someone gives you a quote or tells you something private to help you bid, it is to be kept private. Never reveal or peddle inside information, or make amendments or adjustments to final quotes unless asked by the receiver to do so. Above all DON'T BROADCAST YOUR BID; it is between you and the owners/builders, that is all. Your crew, your suppliers, your spouse, your competitors, your banker, no one needs to know the price before the contract is awarded, and few really need this information afterward. Having your employees running around telling everyone that we are getting $150 per condo for construction cleanup isn't very smart. Even after the job is done, I'd keep the price to yourself and your files. In cleaning there is always a next time, and it is usually to your advantage to keep rates and amounts confidential.

THOSE EXTRA TOUCHES

That make you stand out as "the best," and give extra advantages and future work (which means extra praise and profits).

Wear Uniforms

Look like a professional. Be identifiable. This will work to your advantage many times over. Have a name (yours and your company's) on your uniform. People will trust you more, treat you better, and it's a good discipline for your employees.

Be Findable

Leave a card for the owners that tells where and how to find you.

Take a Lunch

Leaving your job to eat means travel, extra time, and the higher cost of "eating out." Often you can make more profit with a lunch than with a

THE BIDDING TABLE
BEFORE & AFTER!

piece of cleaning equipment. Try to minimize your own breaks during the day, and don't eat or drink in damageable areas or use the client's good tables, chairs, etc.

Do humorous trash runs at lunch time. A five-minute whiz through to police up the fallout from the crews— theirs and yours—goes a long way toward making a good impression.

Park Out of the Way

Keep your trucks and equipment out of everyone's way. Take the worst parking spot even if you are the first ones there. That conveys humility and consideration (that others might have more or heavier stuff to carry, etc.).

Bring Some Traveling Mats

Bring several sets of rubber-backed interior and exterior door mats (with your name on them) to put at doors, inside and out, to keep down tracked in dirt and grit. 3' x 4' or 3' x 5' is a nice size. You can also use these to set your stuff on in case something tips over, or you drip fluid when you're pouring, etc. They not only help keep the place clean, but say "you care."

Make Friends

At the end of a job, the subs and contractors are pushing to get out and the owners are pushing to get in. It is crowded and the movers and decorators believe the cleaners are

in the way. Diplomacy here is almost more valuable than duty fulfillment. "Please," "thank you," "may I help?," "anything more we can do?," and the like will win friends and create more jobs from contractors. This will be the best sales call you can make on a potential new customer.

Share Your Expertise

When anyone inquires what you are using to clean with, take the time to answer or even bring a sample for them. This identifies you as a pro.

Share Your Tools

Leave a couple of nice bottles of cleaning solution and cloths for the owners or the contractors, so they can touch things up if they need to after you are gone. A $20 courtesy here could get you a $2000 job tomorrow.

Avoid Sheep Stealing

During every job, where we work with others and they work with us, there are always transitions of life going on. People complaining, wanting a change, wanting to brag, making projections and plans. All employee ears, of course, are open at all times, and there is opportunity and temptation to steal other people's employees. This is not the time or place to go after or proselytize other people's work force. Do all job offerings and seed-plantings off site. Just a word to the wise, for better public relations and a longer term relationship with the other people involved in a job.

Offer to Seal Concrete

Any exposed interior concrete floors should be sealed with clear finish, to keep them from shedding gritty dust, and make them easy to clean. This step is included in many construction contracts, and you can offer to do it. It will gain you some important extra appreciation (and profit) at little extra cost.

10 TRUTHS OF THE CLEANING PROFESSION

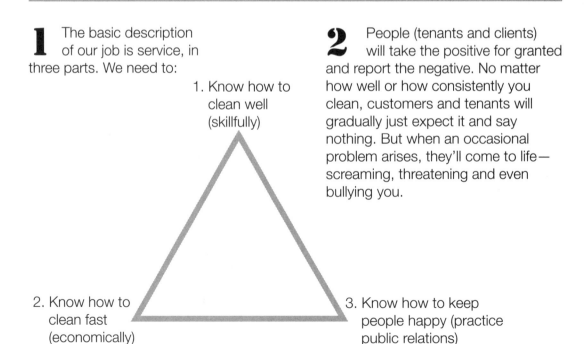

1 The basic description of our job is service, in three parts. We need to:

1. Know how to clean well (skillfully)

2. Know how to clean fast (economically)

3. Know how to keep people happy (practice public relations)

2 People (tenants and clients) will take the positive for granted and report the negative. No matter how well or how consistently you clean, customers and tenants will gradually just expect it and say nothing. But when an occasional problem arises, they'll come to life—screaming, threatening and even bullying you.

3 You can't clean well enough to please someone if they don't like you. If you hate human society, don't get along with people easily, or have any obnoxiousness in your blood, you won't last or be happy in the cleaning industry.

4 This is a lonely business. Off hours, odd shifts and low visibility means your friends and associates, may be limited because in this business you just aren't in circulation much.

5 This is a hands-on business—there's not much room for middle management. You can't just manipulate flunkies and peasants in the ranks. You have to know and be able to do the work yourself to be able to boss it.

6 The biggest reason for failure in the cleaning industry is lack of commitment to the profession. Persistence and endurance are far more valuable than skill or financial backing.

7 In the cleaning field, geography makes little difference, opportunity is everywhere. Dirt is always there—in a big or little town, hot or cold climate. The carpet isn't any cleaner on the other side of the world.

8 We all hire the same people to help us clean—supervision and leadership are the only advantages you have over your competitors.

9 This is a labor-intensive business, and employee turnover is the single greatest cause of customer complaints and management stress. See my book *How to Upgrade & Motivate Your Cleaning Crew* for some good ways to reduce turnover.

10 Lack of work appreciation, not job boredom, is the biggest cause of employee dissatisfaction.

PS. It ain't no fun if you don't make the mun.

REMEMBER

The Single Biggest Plague of Construction Cleanup:

REDOS

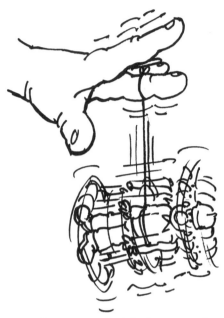

Going back, repeating and recleaning anything kills you because you are generally only getting paid to do it once. Whenever possible, make sure you are the last one out or make sure the last one out leaves the area as clean as they found it.

On the other hand, having or even expecting perfect order and organization in a construction job is idealistic and impossible. When job superintendents decide "it's time" for you and your crews to clean, you go after it, even though there may be some minor finish items not complete, like a faulty light that needs to be replaced, or a few paint nicks, or trim that needs to be touched up. Little pieces of hardware and other things like clamps, rails, and lenses (that have been back-ordered and delayed) will often show up right on opening day, or hours before it. They will need to be installed ASAP and new mounting chips, residue, and dust will follow.

In a situation like this you will often leave the room or unit perfect only to find the next day some other contractor has come behind you and messed it up—and they will. Once you are given a building to clean, it is deemed "yours," no matter who beats it up afterward. No amount of whining, blaming, threats, or refusals will change this. Only good preparation, communication, and **records** will help.

Nothing cuts profits or makes you look more incompetent than not being in control of these unforeseen problems on a construction job (even if they aren't your fault). Check, check, check, and recheck, then respond and deal with any new mess or problems you find, then record (see the following page). Your alertness can and will help others at the job, because toward the end of a job it's kind of an "every man [or woman] for himself" atmosphere.

Some Things That Will Really Help Here:

1. Have the contractor physically label or mark completed work, rooms, and areas. This will be a great deterrent to other trades messing them up again.

2. Require all freight and furnishings to be unpacked on the dock or in the garage— not in the place you've just cleaned.

3. Document all redos and get a signature, like this:

_____/_____/_____
Date cleaned   Area   Signature

_____/_____/_____
Date cleaned   Area   Signature

4. Before leaving, submit a "punch list" or "squawk list." (A list of items or details that are the responsibility of others which you notice are amiss or not complete, may cause a problem, etc.)

We are in the room checking things out when we are finished with it. We are the first to see chipped bathtubs, broken coat racks, missing mirrors, and hot and cold water knobs reversed. Hand your punch list to the contractor's supervisor each night and you just saved him six hours of work and it didn't cost anything!

One thing more needs to be clear in regard to this: when I say "contact" or "report" I don't mean TATTLE.

As I mentioned earlier, when something is amiss (there will be plenty)— lost, ruined, damaged, stolen, or abused, don't hurry into a hostile position. Don't point fingers and accuse. In fact, if you can fix something easily (even if it wasn't your fault), do it and politely inform the pertinent party of your good deed, and word will get around that you are a team player!

Again, when you need to report on problems or shortcomings in a facility, combine your lacks with theirs on a general list rather than a "hang 'em," single-them-out list. Throughout this book I've emphasized the value of "harmony" on a construction job—this is serious stuff. If you make or have enemies at the job site, you'll suffer emotionally, physically, and financially, and it will be your last job there. If, on the other hand, the others on the job like you, they will do much of your work for you and seek you out for future jobs. I've pointed out at least a dozen different ways this comes to bear, when it comes to handling the financial aspects of jobs, the cleanup itself, and all and any coworkers. If you didn't catch them all, re-read the book.

This is a copy of the punch list we use to indicate uncompleted cleaning (or other) tasks:

For Offices and Other Buildings

CONSTRUCTION CLEANUP
PUNCH LIST

VARSITY CONTRACTORS, INC.

Project _____   Date _____

Location _____

ROOM/AREA	WORK COMPLETED	DESCRIPTION OF WORK TO BE COMPLETED	DATE COMPLETED

Inspected by _____   Project Manager _____

An important last task—

THE JOB SHEET

This is one of the most important sheets of paper in your business, even more important than the bid or the check! All it is, is a history and record of the job and must be filled out completely the minute a job is over. If you do this, it will be one of the greatest construction cleanup tools you own.

1. It is a record/document of the job, location, personnel, bid—everything!
2. It records and verifies the workers' time and place on the job.
3. It can help you organize and schedule the job.
4. It can be used (the first half of it) as a bid sheet.
5. It accounts where all the money came from and went.
6. It is an almost perfect profit/loss statement. If you have it filled in correctly, have identified and recorded all the costs, it will be an eye-opening account of what you made or lost on the job.

Read over the filled-in job sheet a couple of times and it will be plain to you why it is so valuable.

Not knowing where you are is one of THE BIGGEST REASONS FOR FAILURE in business. Not the lack of cash, bad work, low bids, poor employees, but **not knowing exactly where you are in income and outgo** is the major reason for failure of businesses like ours.

Now, here is the best reason to always make and keep a job sheet on every job. You will get similar, and sometimes almost exactly the same, jobs to do again, and all you have to do is grab the job sheet and it will tell you what happened, how long it took, what to watch out for, etc. As I mentioned a few pages ago, the history or record of a job done, one that you personally completed, is one of the best bidding resources going.

On the following page is the job sheet I use for my operations. You can copy it, or send a postcard with your name and address and we will send you an 8 1/2 x 11 clean black and white original. Or look at this one and make up your own by adjusting this to the specifics of your situation. Just leave the space for what you need to keep track of. And never, never, NEVER do a job without a job sheet filled in, **honestly**.

Job Sheet

	CODE	AREA/REGION	CONTACT	BID	SCHEDULE	COMPLETED	BILLED	PAID	TICKLER TIME
JOB SHEET	Tag-wood	Idaho	Marshall	7/15/15	OK	8/7/15	8/8/15	9/15/15	Next Yr

1 Contact

Client	Marshall Developments Inc
Contact	Jon Marshall
Address	1291 West Field
City/ST/ZIP	Pocatello, ID 83203

☐ New ☐ Existing ☒ Commercial ☐ Residential

Position: Owner/manager
Phone: 208-233-7300 cell 208-241-9280
Fax: 208-233-7301

2 Acct. Info

☒ SAME AS ABOVE   Billing Phone _____

Client _____
Billing Address _____
City/ST/ZIP _____

☐ Bill PO # _____   ☐ MasterCard ☐ VISA ☐ Check Enclosed
Credit Card # _____
Expiration Date _____
Card Holder Signature _____

3 Job Prep

Equipment Needed:
- ☐ Pressure washer
- ☐ 2 lb extension ladder
- ☐
- ☐
- ☐
- ☐

Supplies Needed:
- ☐
- ☐
- ☐
- ☐
- ☐

Safety Check:
- ☐ 4 cones/driveway
- ☐ Hard hats required
- ☐

Special Notes: Will be news media walking through.

Key Schedule: Will be issued to Varsity

4 Bid

Job Description:

Construction clean up of ISU campus academic building as per attached specifications.

Job Location: City/campus   Bid By: Don Aslett
Contact Location: City/campus   Unit Costs: S.F.
Scheduled: August 1-15   Colors: —
Access: Total

Authorized Total Cost: **$1435**

5 Job Cost $

LABOR	PAY RATE	Aug 2	Aug 3	Aug 4	Aug 8	TOTAL HOURS	TOTAL PAY
Boss: Don A.	25	4	2	2	2	10	250
Arnold S.	10	0	8	8	0	16	160
Dave H.	8	0	8	7	0	15	120
Denny J.	8	0	8	5	2	15	120
Hank C.	8	0	4	4	0	8	64

Describe additional work:

Hauled 1 load of trash at Jon's request — $50

Helped move and unload 2 hrs @ $15 — $30

Paid _____ Ck # _____   Add'l Amount **$80.00**

Labor Burden

AL 15%	NE 15%
AK 21%	NV 18%
AZ 14%	NM 16%
AR 16%	NJ 15%
CA 26%	NY 23%
CO 17%	NC 15%
CT 15%	ND 10%
FL 18%	OH 23%
GA 16%	OK 18%
ID 15%	OR 16%
IA 16%	PA 27%
IL 18%	SC 17%
IN 15%	SD 15%
KS 17%	TN 17%
KY 19%	TX 24%
MD 14%	UT 15%
MA 13%	VA 15%
MI 20%	WA 12%
MN 17%	WI 19%
MO 18%	WY 15%
MT 26%	

Total Labor 714
+ Labor Burden 142.80

EXPENSES						Total Expenses
Vehicle .45/mi	30	60	30	30	67.50	
Equip Rental	---	40	40	---	80.00	
Lunch	---	26	---	12	38.00	
Cleaner	31	---	---	---	31.00	
Calls	18	---	---	---	18.00	
Other Towels	5	---	8	---	13.00	
Other Tarp cover	---	---	39	---	39.00	
Other Misc.	6	5	3.20	---	14.20	
Total Expenses					300.70	

Total Income **$ 1515.00**

Overhead=10% of Total Income — 151.50

856.80

300.70

Total Expenses $ 1309.00

Estimated Profit/Loss $ 206.00

6 Follow-Up

Completed	Signed	Recall #	Copies Out	Customer Delight
8/7/15	J Marshall	---	OK	😊 😊 😐 😞

For a free 8x11 original of this blank form, send a POSTCARD with your name and address to Job Sheet, PO Box 700, Pocatello ID 83204.

The Mechanics of It All:

EQUIPMENT

One real positive of construction cleanup is that it doesn't take much equipment or many supplies. The key is have the **right** stuff—**right there**.

Make sure it's:

Available

Never be on a construction job where you have to "run and get" something. The key to a fast and profitable job is to have everyone working all the time. So always have the right size equipment and the products you need.

I favor #2 below. It requires a little more equipment but produces a lot more **accountability**. It keeps things organized, pinpoints any blame, and also eliminates the setting of wet containers of chemicals on desktops (or other surfaces), resulting in ring stains. There are lots of choices of styles of caddies, and tool boxes can also be used.

Equipping your crew on the site and on the job

You have two choices here:

1. All of you work out of a central supply.

2. Each individual has his or her own cleaning caddy.

Large caddy

5-gallon bucket with tool holder

Large open-face tool box

Make Sure It's Marked

Twice! And BIG! Have your equipment branded with a name and maybe even a logo or patch of bright-colored paint; this will retard the pilferage that can occur even while you are on the job. Other subs, for example, will "borrow" your buckets even while you are using them. Heavily identified property has a way of staying put—MARK everything before you start the job! Keep an inventory of your major items and don't use your expensive or top-of-the-line equipment on a construction cleanup job.

Make Sure It's Safely Stored

Never leave any of your equipment on or around the job or construction site. Everything is fair game and will be gone if you do. Bring it to the job and take it with you at the end of the day.

You can work out of your car, but an older van or pickup with a lockable shell is perfect. Remember that most of the time the vehicle is parked, and you are just using it as a mobile storage unit, so you can have an older inexpensive one. Be sure your well-identified ladder can fit inside! It is also an advantage to have a private place like this to eat lunch or make calls, but the best thing is that you'll have your material handy when you need it.

On-site Storage of Equipment

The ideal is to have a lockable covered pickup or van to carry your equipment and supplies to and from the job, and to work out of it at the job site. This is the way to do it. It eliminates risks, accidents, thievery, and wasted time. However, many construction cleanup jobs are done in sequence as groups of units are finished—the job might span a month or two and you will leave a crew on the job or allow them to come there with their own vehicles (or by bus or foot) and work. In this case, you won't have to show up every morning and evening to load and haul—you can just keep your material, safety gear, and supplies at the job site.

If you have occasion to do this, it might be wise to search out or build a storage unit. It needs to be something strong, lockable, versatile, and semi-portable. Above all, it needs to be weatherproof, and I'll even say make it metal so it is unburnable. Put your name on it in bold display type and label it "Cleaning Gear" and most people will leave it alone. Who wants to steal a mop and broom when there are Skilsaws and socket sets around?

These also make a nice central, permanent unit to work out of and can be

placed in a central spot and moved to other places as the job progresses. It's cheaper than a van and driver, too.

Rental

For "one time" operations or special applications it is often better to rent than to own the equipment. The rental charge itself is never the "expensive" part of this. It's the picking it up and taking it back. Don't forget that when you're making comparisons and analyses. Keeping something a few days or a week longer than the agreed-on time is always a mistake. It is a careless way to cut profit. Your goal with rental equipment is to return it fast! Waiting will usually mean lost time and money.

Their Equipment

(The other subcontractors', that is) is always a bigger problem than yours. It's forever in the way. They find corners, closets, walls, and floor space to stash and pile their buckets and other tools and it is always where you need to clean. Moving their stuff out of or around the room can take longer than the cleaning you are there to do, and you won't get paid for this. You may also be accused of misplacing or breaking their equipment. Before you start a job, demand a clean and clear area, or charge extra to move things when you clean. You can also gracefully refuse to clean the area until removal is complete.

Your Construction Cleanup

SHOPPING
LIST

You will use most of this stuff. It pays to have some extra here because often, other subs will ask for some of yours to clean their own area.

The amount or number you need of each of the following depends on the size of the job and size of crew—be sure to match it so that everyone is fully "armed."

All of this is common cleaning gear that you can get at the local janitorial supply store. If your local supplier doesn't have something, write to me for a free catalog/newsletter that has what you need. Send a postcard to:

Clean Report
PO Box 700-Cons
Pocatello ID 83204
Don@Aslett.com

Exterior Cleanup

You'll notice that on most bids, proposals, and billings the word "interior" is used over and over. Generally the only outside construction cleanup you'll be asked to do is the outside of windows; the rest is all inside. For some reason, the landscaping people usually get the call to clean/clear the exterior. BUT be sure to ask the people on the job site what they want done on the outside, if anything. And make it clear that you could do it. It is good business to suggest exterior cleanup whenever you can. If a client does want you to do it, just be sure it is included in your proposal, bid, and schedule.

Possible exterior work:

1. Windows (generally included in your jobs)
2. Policing and removal of trash and debris
3. Cleaning planters/planting splatters on the lower part of buildings
4. Pressure washing of walks and driveways
5. Removal of spills, drips, spots, and marks from same
6. Striping or other marking of parking lots
7. Removal of signs, posters, staples, tape, etc., from poles, etc., on the premises
8. Mowing or spraying of weeds

Equipment List

- ❏ your own trash container(s)
- ❏ drop cloths (canvas)
- ❏ complete window-cleaning kit:
    - ❏ extension pole
    - ❏ washing wand
    - ❏ squeegee
    - ❏ extra squeegee blades
    - ❏ sponge
    - ❏ razor scraper
    - ❏ cloths
    - ❏ dish washing liquid such as Joy
- ❏ backpack vacuum
- ❏ upright vacuum (with beater bar)
- ❏ wet-dry vacuum with a long hose and wide mouth attachment
- ❏ push brooms/counter brooms
- ❏ dustpans (at least 2)
- ❏ dustmop(s)
- ❏ dust treat
- ❏ microfiber cloths or treated dust-cloths
- ❏ lambswool dusting wand
- ❏ mop set
    - ❏ bucket
    - ❏ wringer
    - ❏ mop
- ❏ Scrubbee Doo or "Doodlebug"
- ❏ cleaning cloths (see page 66)
- ❏ all-purpose cleaner
- ❏ De-Solv-it® or Delimonene label remover
- ❏ grout cleaner
- ❏ spray bottles
- ❏ plastic scrapers
- ❏ putty knives
- ❏ scrub pads
    - ❏ blue   ❏ white

- ❏ caddies or work aprons (at least 2)
- ❏ buckets (at least 4)
- ❏ safety sign(s)
- ❏ furniture polish
- ❏ floor finish
- ❏ ladder(s)
- ❏ ladder pads
- ❏ extension cords
- ❏ personal protective equipment
    - ❏ rubber gloves
    - ❏ goggles
    - ❏ ear plugs
    - ❏ dust masks
- ❏ work aprons
- ❏ trash can liners
- ❏ measuring tape
- ❏ first aid kit
- ❏ flashlights
- ❏ lunch/cooler of water and disposable cups
- ❏ hour cards

Exterior Options

- ❏ wheelbarrow or utility cart(s)
- ❏ pressure nozzle or washer
- ❏ rake(s)
- ❏ shovel(s)
    - ❏ regular
    - ❏ flat nose

- ❏ _____
- ❏ _____
- ❏ _____
- ❏ _____
- ❏ _____

Spray Bottles

Spray bottles allow you to apply cleaning solution a lot faster than you can with a cloth and make it easier to reach all the nooks and crannies. They keep your hands out of harsh chemicals, too. Best of all, when you buy your cleaners in concentrated form and dilute them into reusable spray bottles, you save money and bottle lugging, and reduce packaging waste.

Pro spray bottles from your janitorial supply store will last longer than discount brands and they're bigger, too, usually a full quart, so you won't run out as often. Plus, the bottles have a good-size base to stand on so they won't tip over easily. Choose see-through bottles so you can color code your cleaners. Not only is this safer, but it speeds things up when you can see the glass cleaner is blue, disinfectant cleaner pink, and all-purpose cleaner green.

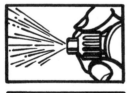

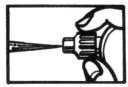

To make the most of your spray cleaning, be sure to adjust the nozzle to the job at hand. A fine spray is great for covering large areas, but you don't want to use too fine a mist in an enclosed area such as a shower, or you'll be inhaling a lot of superfine cleaning solution. The coarse spray setting puts more solution on the surface faster, and the semi-mist setting is what you want to spritz on such things as dirty handprints to prevent the cleaner from running down the wall. When storing spray bottles filled with chemicals, always turn the nozzles to off and tighten them down to prevent leakage.

Professional Cleaning Cloths

The cleaning cloth made of terry toweling is probably the most important tool on a construction cleanup job. Not just for its absorbency but its flexibility (the many different jobs it can do—wiping, streak-free drying, buffing, and dusting).

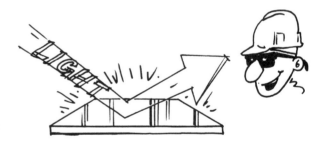

Here is a principle to remember in cleaning ALL of the surfaces described hereafter.

Shine, that big important part of the image of "clean," is created by light hitting a surface and bouncing off.

If residue of any kind is left (even on a clean, sanitary surface) the light that hits the surface will be absorbed, resulting in a dull appearance

This means that all the surfaces we are cleaning (sinks, tubs, woodwork, stainless, etc.), need to be wiped and polished dry after they are washed, so the surface is left at its maximum reflectability. THIS is the most important thing a cleaning cloth can and will do for you.

Just remember that you want the right kind of cleaning cloth. Forget about the "rags" we hoard for the purpose. They're full of lint, seams, buttons, zippers, and holes, and worst of all, often made of materials that fail to absorb or may even repel water. Rags like these are fine for cleaning your hands when you're painting—period.

Cotton terry cloth, on the other hand, is ultra absorbent, and all the little nubs on the terry cloth not only dry things fast, but can reach down into textured surfaces. Terry is strong enough to protect your hands while you're working with it on tough jobs, too.

When you finish with your cloths, don't just toss them into a pile somewhere and leave them or they'll get stiff and ruined. Run them through the washer and then tumble them dry and they'll be ready to work wonders for you again when you need them.

Here's how to make your own cleaning cloths. Get some heavy cotton terry cloth, preferably white (old towels are fine for the purpose) and cut it into 18"x18" squares. Hem all the edges of each square and fold it over once. Then sew the long side together firmly and you'll have a tube of terry. Fold it once, and then again, and it'll just fit your hand. As you use it, it can be folded and refolded and then turned inside out to give you 16 fresh sides to clean with.

You can also purchase ready-made pro cleaning cloths from my Cleaning Center.

Fold finished cloth to fit your hand, approx. 4" x 9".

CLEANING
1 • 2 • 3 • 4

Four Basic Steps of Pro Cleaning

Eliminate

Just as we sweep a floor before we mop it, scrape the dishes before we wash them, clear the counter before we attempt to clean it—apply this principle in all your cleaning. Brush or vacuum, etc. all the crumbs, dust, litter and debris away before you clean. Why end up with all that stuff in your cleaning water, or take a chance of spreading stains? Before you start wetting anything down or going after stuck-on or embedded soil, remove all the big stuff and anything loose.

Saturate

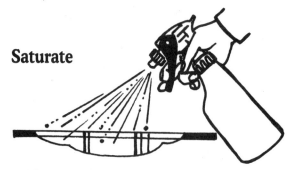

Now put the chemicals to work for you. Spread, wipe, mop, or spray the cleaning solution on the surface. Be sure to apply enough to keep the surface wet enough for the chemicals to work, but not so much that it floods and runs. Then let the solution have time to do its job, to soak in and break down and dissolve the dirt and grime. The harder it works, the less you have to.

Agitate

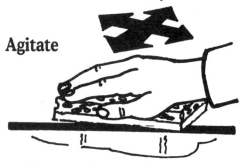

Cleaning often needs some movement, too, to help loosen the dirt or even just to move it off and away. This is "agitation," as when the agitator in a washing machine churns the soil off our clothes. The everyday word for it is scrubbing, and we do it only when we need to, and with a tool to fit the job (cloth, nylon pad, brush, etc.).

Remove

REMOVE now all the soil and solution, which we can accomplish by rinsing, wiping with a cloth or sponge, squeegeeing, using a wet/dry vac, whatever it takes to get EVERYTHING (dirt, soil, moisture, soap residue) off the surface.

Cleaning Chemicals

Always Know

What you're using. We are often cleaning with chemicals... and for our own good, our health and life, not just the job we're doing, we need to know what those chemicals are and what they do. That green liquid can be all-purpose cleaner, quaternary ammonia, or isopropyl alcohol—all used on different things at different times for different reasons. You've got to know the cleaners you use regularly as well as you know your favorite foods: what they contain and what they help and hurt. So STUDY UP and what you don't know, MSDS Material Safety Data Sheets, spec sheets, labels, brochures, or a salesperson can enlighten you about. You're the one who's going to be using these things—you need to educate yourself.

Read the Directions

Amazing, the amount of information that's right there on the label. The Whats, Hows, Wheres, and What Ifs are all spelled out. Yet not one in 50 of us takes the time (all of 30 seconds) to read and learn what we have here and where to use it, what to do and what not to do. Directions are our road map when we're traveling, and when we tackle a cleaning job, they tell us how to save both building surfaces and our lives. Manufacturers know their chemicals but they can only let us in on what they know if we take the time to read and study. DO IT.

Be a 100% direction reader.

Use Proper Dilutions

More isn't always better—the dilution ratio has a lot to do with a cleaning solution's ability to dissolve and suspend the dirt. When you use too much chemical, or too little, you defeat the whole purpose of the chemical, lessen its dissolving ability, do poor work, waste time, and damage surfaces (if not people).

60 to 1 for example, means 60 cups of water to a cup of cleaner. The average bucket holds 36 cups of water. That means in this case you'd be adding no more than a half cup of cleaner. A 20 to 1 solution would be a lot stronger.

I know we don't always have the time and means to measure, so we have to "glug-glug," but if we pay close attention the first few times to EXACTLY how much we put in, it'll be a lot easier to hit the mark next time without measuring. Pre-measured packets of cleaner concentrate, available from the Cleaning Center and janitorial-supply stores, are a big help here.

When you're mixing, remember: Too little baking soda in the biscuits means they won't rise; too much ruins them. The same with cleaners—measure your chemicals, don't guess... too much detergent makes your job harder and creates problems.

POST your MSDS (Material Safety Data Sheets) so everyone knows what a chemical is, what's in it, and what to do if it happens to be misused or spilled, accidentally gets in or on us.

A Few More Important Facts About Cleaning

Moisture

Or WATER is needed for most cleaning and it seldom hurts a surface if it's only in contact with it for a short time. Left on there too long, however, moisture will work its way into and swell and damage many surfaces. Remember, too, that as water evaporates, the active ingredients in your cleaning solution may double and triple in strength. This is especially true of ammoni-ated products. When in doubt, get the cleaning solution on and off quickly—better safe than sorry.

Drying

Has to be done right. If something dries too fast it may not do a thorough job of cleaning, or (in the case of something like wax) bond well to the surface; if it dries too slow, having the moisture on there so long will warp and rot things. YOU are in control here, so remember: air movement and air circulation (especially of outside air) will dry things faster than still dead air at 100 degrees. Even cool outside air will dry things faster than still inside air. When washing windows, walls, and floors, slow drying is best—for carpet and upholstery, the faster the better.

Go Easy!

"Scrub," "scour," "elbow grease," and "cleanser" are militant, violent words in the cleaning vocabulary. Professionals lift, dissolve, and pull off soils, ease and rinse them away. Too often when we come across a stubborn soil we attack it by pushing harder with meaner tools.

"WET" is the key word here. Keep any surface you need to assert yourself on wet. This will soften the soil and lubricate the surface if you have to do any rubbing or scrubbing, so the soil will generally give up before the surface gives out.

SWEEPING

Sweeping means removing dust and loose dirt and debris.

What you need

1. dustmop or broom
2. hand broom and dust pan
3. a putty knife to scrape up gum or tar

How to do it

1. In aisles and corridors, a straight end-to-end sweeping method is best. In open areas, dust mop in a side-to-side pattern with the

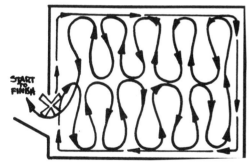

same edge of the mop always leading, and never lift the mop off the floor. A dust mop is light and mobile enough to operate one-handed so the other hand is free to move chairs, and other objects. This will increase your production 40%! Hold the mop in your right hand, move furniture with your left, and work from right to left for greatest efficiency.

2. Use your hand broom to clean out corners, behind furnishings, and floor edges.

3. As you accumulate dirt, sweep it into a pile (not a long row), and use your hand broom to sweep it into the dust pan and dispose of it. I like small portable dust pans and foxtail pickup brooms or "counter brushes."

4. Dust mops should be brushed out after use and lightly re-treated with dust mop treat. Change heads as needed. After washing, dust mop heads should be sprayed with dust mop treat and placed in a plastic bag for 24 hours to reabsorb treatment before using. Rental dust mops come ready to use. Never store dust mops on the floor or against walls, or the surface will suck the oil treatment out of the mop and make a stain.

Professional Secrets of Better, Faster

VACUUMING

Always police the area first, to get any large debris off the carpet. A quick bend to pick up an object by hand is a lot faster and smarter than wasting ten minutes—and who knows how much repair shop money—trying to dig it out of your vacuum.

When possible, plug in to a strategic location that will allow you to vacuum the maximum area and avoid backtracking.

Slow, deliberate strokes pick up better and are faster in the end than zipping over one area three or four times. Let the vacuum work for you. It needs time for the beater bar to loosen the dirt and for the air flow to suck it up. If you watch a lot of vacuumers, you'll see that much time is spent in overlap. This is a waste of time if you

have a beater brush assembly on your vacuum. Overlap each stroke an inch or so, but avoid running the machine over the same area twice, except as might be needed in badly soiled, high-traffic areas.

If you have a room that's especially dirty, you may have to resort to overlapping, up and back vacuuming strokes. But this takes a lot of time, tires you out, and usually isn't necessary. In rooms or halls that are too small for effective maneuvering, instead push

the vacuum to the end of the stroke and then pull it back to cover the next strip of carpet. After you've pulled the vacuum all the way back, push it forward again and repeat the process. This method is quick and will do an effective job 90 percent of the time.

Always keep your vacuum on carpeted area while it's running. You can ruin a beautiful wood floor, for example, by running a low-adjusted beater bar type vacuum over it. The metal part of the bar will thump the floor on every rotation and dent it (at great expense to you, since your insurance covers liability but not stupidity).

Beware of

BUILDING INJURY!

Almost everything you will be cleaning will be NEW, whether you are cleaning up after a remodeling job or new construction. The owners will expect perfection when they see it. But too often those of us putting the finishing touches on a building, fixing or installing something in it—or cleaning it—do much damage with our carts, chemicals, and equipment. Snippets of wire, dropped screws, nails, staples, or packing residue will be left on the floor or in the tub and will get stepped on or dragged around, gouging or chipping a perfectly new

A BIG REMINDER

AGAIN...

Construction cleanup is a DIFFERENT kind of cleaning, not the old scrubbing and scraping away of buildups of grease, wax, hard water deposits, animal stains, etc. So, you'll not be using much heavy duty equipment: high powered cleaning machines, powerful cleaners, harsh brushes and pads. Construction cleanup is almost a job you could do in a business suit, by comparison—where you police, not plow the place clean. Construction cleanup will go quickly if...

1. The area is clear and ready for you.

2. You have the right and **enough** equipment on hand.

surface before the clients ever touch a finger to it. Spilled chemicals, or coffee or other drinks, cigarettes, etc., from the workers often mar facilities more during the final stages of construction than the occupant will in many years of use. Moving furniture or other big, heavy items in and out can easily scar door casings, walls, and doors. Ladders and scaffolding carried in and out or leaned up against something the wrong way, or anchored wrong on a floor can leave permanent damage.

For example, electricians let snippings of wire fall to the bottom of a tub or the floor and a 200-pound craftsman tromps and grinds them

into the finish, damaging it. You come along afterward and try to clean these problems away. You can't, but do get blamed for "scratching it."

Or another example: tile or carpet installers (generally about the last to work on a house) flip or drag something against expensive wall coverings or cherry woodwork and make cuts or gouges.

There are hundreds of possibilities for accidental injury involving glass, fixtures, tile, paint, mountings, and more.

You will see a lot of this when cleaning up behind construction workers and you need to report it, point it out immediately to the job site boss.

Any major or minor injury to a building has to be fixed—someone has to fix it, someone has to pay. See to it that it isn't you (us!) that damages, doing the cleaning.

You always want to answer for your own errors and pay for them, but not for others' mistakes.

DAMAGE DANGER:
This is a BIG factor! Play it smart now or you'll pay plenty later.

WHEN YOU BID A JOB & SEE DAMAGE —NOTE IT

WHEN YOU FIND DAMAGE— DOCUMENT & REPORT IT

WHEN YOU CAUSE DAMAGE— NOTE & REPORT IT IMMEDIATELY!

Dealing with
DUST

Most people believe that "dusty" is another word for "old." Those people have obviously never been to a construction site.

Construction dust outdoes all other dust. You have:

- sheetrock dust
- sawdust
- sanding dust
- concrete dust
- metal cutting dust
- packing and unpacking dust
- landscaping dust (generally the landscaping of the grounds won't be complete before your final cleanup and that means wind and heavy foot traffic will be bringing yard dust into the building)

All of this dust is in the air and all over the place and it's still there, on and inside everything, even after the builders have left.

Dust is the first thing you go for after the trash and leftover construction materials are gone.

This is critical now…

Where and when possible—VAC-UUM it away!

You need a good vacuum with a long wand and brush nozzles, or a backpack vac.

Start high, and work your way from the ceiling down. Don't be fooled. Dust is everywhere—on light fixtures, grilles, slide tracks, vents, even on walls.

Vacuum all door and window frames above the floor area (tank vacs are good for this). However use beater bar vacuums on the carpet. The dust on the carpet is deeper than you think and needs to be agitated and bounced out.

Do walls with a soft, brush nozzle. After vacuuming, all hard surfaces need a final wipedown with a mi-crofiber or treated dust cloth (see following).

A heavy push broom is great for removing larger debris: hunks, scraps, clippings and "pieces" of all kinds, but a treated dustmop is what you want to corral fine dirt, silt, and dust on floors. I often use a dustmop several times in the course of a job—they are FAST

and effective. Be especially sure to use a dustmop prior to mopping; it will remove residue and keep your mop water clean!

How to Treat Dust Mops and cloths

Any dust mop or untreated cloth needs to be treated with "dust treat" so it will be able to pick up and hold even the finest dust and dirt.

Apply the dust treat according to the directions, being sure to use the right amount, not too much or too little, for the size of mop or cloth you have. Give the treatment time to really soak into the mop or cloth before you use it. Apply the treatment and then wrap the head or cloth up in a plastic bag and let it sit overnight. Once the mop or cloth is in use you'll have to add a little more treat from time to time, to keep it at full pickup power.

P.S. Don't store your dust mops in bags just sitting around somewhere because bags around the job get thrown out!

WINDOWS

Windows and glass are "THE" major items in construction cleanup. They are unpredictable as to the extent of foreign matter or debris on them. Overspray of sealer onto exterior windows, for instance, can up the time required to clean them by over 400%. Windows with mortar, paint, and labels also mean you will have to do more than just wash them. Here is some window wisdom for construction cleanup.

Glass cleaning is far more complex than the undertrained crew member might believe.

It is not uncommon for a single 5 x 7 foot polarized window panel to cost $400-$600 plus labor to replace. With the wrong acid or a razor scraper, a well-meaning worker can do damage into six-figure dollar numbers in a matter of days. Remember: if you ruin it, you pay to replace it.

Construction window cleaning jobs are unique. Many professional window washers will not get involved in bidding them. They realize a miscalculation here is far more costly than on ordinary, easy, frequently cleaned windows. Most, also, are not well informed on the full range of methods that may be called for, making them uneasy in a bid.

Glass has many different compositions, with varying degrees of hardness and flexibility. This is why, if any doubt or question arises, you need to get the care label from the installer. Plexiglas, for instance (which is actually plastic), is extremely soft and almost all standard window-cleaning methods will scratch or discolor it. The best way to clean Plexiglas is usually with cheesecloth and a special cleaner formulated for Plexiglas. It cleans, as well as removes or minimizes existing scratches. Other types of soft glass may require special handling also, especially if using razor scrapers. So if you don't know about a certain mirror or glass, get specs.

The color or coating of the glass must be taken into account here, too. There are four main kinds of glass we come up against here:

1. Colored glass

2. Glass with reflective coating

3. Glass with polarized coating

4. Polarized glass

Colored glass is not usually a problem, but the others are very delicate. When cleaning glass with coatings, you need to ascertain exactly what the manufacturer suggests.

When inspecting glass, it is important to note what kind of framework and finish has been used around the windows. Painted areas need to be watched even when using regular window cleaner, or long streaks of discolored paint may result. In construction cleanup especially, keep the solution on the glass as much as possible, and don't flood the window with cleaner.

Suggested Procedure

Observe and ask about any glass you're not familiar with, especially if it has color, texture, coating, or a strange frame. Ask the contractor if there are manufacturer specs for the cleaning and care of the window. Even dumb questions save some stupid mistakes. Be smart **before** you start. It also reduces your liability if something happens.

Get the bulk of the dirt off the windows first—remember this is the first time they have been cleaned and glass and frames collect dust and dirt, inside and out. They generally aren't ready to be finish-cleaned.

Vacuum around frames, inside and out, to pull chips and snips and settled sanding dust out of the tracks and frame corners. If you don't do this, all this debris will be floating in your cleaning water and streak the glass. Or it will turn your cleaning water to mud. Either way the windows will take 10 times longer to clean. Really dirty outside windows can be hosed down quickly to get rid of mud, cobwebs, bird deposits, etc.

Now, do your first-pass washing. For this you want to have a bucket full of cleaning solution (water with a bit of all-purpose cleaner in it), a squeegee, a wash and pickup sponge, and an empty bucket. Bathe the windows with a sponge wetted in the cleaning solution until they are slick and soapy. Keep them wet and don't scrub—just wash them gently. When your sponge gets dirty, squeeze it into the empty bucket. Use the squeegee to wipe the solution off the windows when you're done. Delabel the windows (see page 85).

Finish-clean them. Equipment needed for this (all of which you can find at a janitorial-supply store):

● 12 or 14" professional quality brass squeegee such as the Ettore

● window wand or scrubber such as the Golden Glove

● bucket of cleaning solution (see below)

● extension pole if you're doing high windows

Squeegeeing in Short:

Don't let the idea of it intimidate you. All you do is apply cleaning solution with the wand or a sponge, and then remove it (along with all the dirt) with the squeegee.

1 Wipe around the outside edge of the window with a damp cloth to remove any debris that otherwise might get caught under your squeegee blade.

2 Mix up your solution: Not more than a few drops of liquid dish detergent (I like Joy) in a bucket of warm water. Any more cleaner than that will only cause streaking.

3 Dip the flat side of the scrubber (or a sponge) just about 1/4 inch into the solution and wet the window lightly. Then go back over it to loosen any stubborn soil, and run your scrubber

quickly around the window against the frame to pick up any dirt you may have shoved against it.

 Before you start squeegee-ing, wet the blade of the squeegee with a damp cloth, so it won't skip and jump around on the glass. Wipe the blade between strokes, too, when you're working with it.

 Tilt the squeegee so that only about an inch of the blade rests lightly against the top of the window.

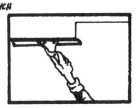

Then pull it straight across the top to create a dry strip about an inch wide. This will prevent those mad-dening drops from running down from the top.

 Put the squeegee blade in the dry area and pull it down to about 3 inches from the bottom of the window. Repeat until the

whole window is done, be-ing sure to overlap a little into the last stroke each time to keep water from running into the already clean area.

Run the squeegee along the bottom of the window to remove the accumulated water and wipe the sill with a dry cloth.

Resist the temptation to remove any lingering water drops or little marks along the frame, etc., with a cloth. Just let them dry and fade away or if you must wipe, use the tip of your bare finger (by now it will be oil-free, and the perfect touchup tool!).

- Don't clean windows in direct sunlight—they'll dry too fast and streak.
- With some windows, you may want to "cut the water" off the sides as well as the top, and then squeegee the rest of the window with horizontal strokes.

● Small decorative panes are best done with a spray bottle of window cleaner and a cleaning cloth or paper towel (not old newspapers!).

MIRRORS

Don't over wet or flood mirrors. It won't hurt the front (which is glass), but when the solution drips off the bottom lip and creeps up the dry silver oxide on the back of mirrors, often the ammoniated, alcohol-based, or whatever cleaner you are using here will do damage (cause permanent black blemishes). For this reason, it's best to not sponge cleaning solution on, or otherwise apply it to a mirror directly, but to spray it on a cloth and then apply the cloth to the mirror, wipe, and buff dry.

Also, **make sure** the mirror is hung or mounted tight and solid before you apply muscle pressure. For some reason, mirrors are often installed rather daintily and will fall off, or move around and scratch walls, etc., when we attempt to clean them.

Finally, watch that you don't leave any lint or wisps of cleaning cloth on the side mounting clamps. Just step back and take a good look before you leave!

BATHROOMS

Bathrooms are a critical part of post-construction cleanup. They take the longest, are expensive to clean, and have the most potential for damage.

The process of cleaning a new hotel, home, or building to the point of ready for occupancy is exciting, but it is also tough. When walking through a place bidding it, you need to look hard. In bathrooms, look for the following areas that could be a problem.

Toilets and bathroom fixtures— do they have labels on them and how hard are they to remove?

Mirrors—do they have protective rubber pads stuck to them? Is there line-up ink or construction debris on the mirrors?

Vanities—Are they marble or Formica? Do they have a smooth surface or a rough surface? How dirty are they?

Plumbing fixtures—are they real chrome or plastic?

There are totally different cleaning requirements here than the usual bathroom attack on hard water deposits, odor, and built-up soap scum. Have the craftspeople leave the bathroom in as good a shape as possible before you get there.

Labels—See page 86.

Caulk Tape—wet carefully and remove with a razor blade.

Grout Slop—wet and chip out with a fingernail or a sharp scraper.

Pencil/Chalk marks—wash off with all-purpose cleaner and a white nylon-faced sponge.

Fixtures—Clean all installed fixtures with a white nylon-backed sponge dampened in all-purpose cleaning solution and buff dry with a cleaning cloth.

Tile—Clean tile with all-purpose cleaner and remove any grout and glue with a wet razor blade. Leave cover pads in tubs while working on the tile.

Sinks—Clean like any other fixture.

Tub—this is the most time-consuming item in the room. It has usually been used as a dumping ground for the following:

cement and plaster chips
wallpaper scraps
glue
sheetrock scraps
wrappers
compounds
grout
things you will never be
  able to identify

Often, you find all of these in a tub, so always be sure to sweep or vacuum the tub out first before cleaning it with water. If something is stuck on there, wet it first, soak it well, and then gently scrape it off.

Floors—damp mop with all purpose cleaner. Generally floors don't need major scrubbing and can be done with a hand tool like the Scrubbee Doo (see page 83).

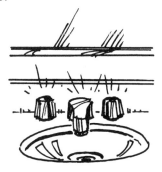

DAMP MOPPING

What you need

1. "Wet Floor" signs

2. mop bucket (buckets with 3" casters are best) with wringer, half-filled with neutral floor cleaner solution

3. empty bucket and wringer

4. mop (I like a 24 oz. head).

How to do it

1 SAFETY FIRST! Before you do anything else, mark the area well with "Wet Floor" signs.

2 Be sure the floor has been swept, dust mopped, or vacuumed well before applying water, and move any furniture, etc., you can out of the way.

3 Now get the mop bucket half-filled with cleaning solution and the empty bucket into which you will wring the dirty water. Dip the mop into the solution bucket, and wring it out almost dry. (When you wring

watch the mop handle so you don't break anything, such as a light fixture overhead.)

4 The way we mop is a lot like coloring with crayons—outline the area first and then fill in the middle. Run the mop all around the outside of the room or area in one continuous stroke. Then use a figure "8" pattern to fill in the middle.

Outlining first prevents water from being slopped up onto the walls and the

figure 8 helps make sure that every bit of floor is gone over twice. The first stroke wets the surface and dissolves the dirt, and the overlapping stroke picks up the loosened dirt. This pattern covers an arm's span of floor at a time, so you can complete each section without walking. Move backwards as you mop, working from the back of the room to the front.

 5 When the mop is dirty on one side, flop it over to the clean side. When both sides are dirty wring the dirty water out into the empty bucket. Don't dip a dirty mop into the cleaning solution without wringing it first, or the solution will quickly turn muddy and ineffective.

6 Keep your mop water clean. Change it as often as needed. You should be able to see a quarter dropped in the bottom of the bucket—if you can't, the water needs changing! If you see a film or mop streaks on the floor after it dries, you're either using too much chemical in the water or mopping with dirty water.

Clean your bucket, wringer and mop thoroughly afterward and store your mop so that it will air dry.

My Favorite Floor Tool!
SCRUBBEE DOO
(or Doodlebug):

Swivel action head has gripper teeth underneath to grab and hold pads, yet peel off easily.

Microfiber pads dust, damp mop, soak up spills, and are safe on every surface.

Scrub pads for every job!

White: light duty cleaning, tub, bathroom tile, glass, etc.; Blue: no wax floor, tile, walls, etc.; Brown: heavy-duty stripping, concrete floors, etc.

And the Wax Applicator pad assures a smooth and shiny finish!

APPLIANCES

For once in appliance-cleaning-history this is not a degreasing job! 98% of the appliances you're cleaning in construction work will be new. Any damage to them will be there from installation—craftspeople bumping, dropping, or sitting things on them .... or you cleaning them. Your procedure with appliances is:

1. Whenever possible, clean appliance areas first before the appliances are installed.

2. Dust the item, vacuum behind, under, inside it, etc.

3. Remove any exposed labels or strip bonding glues.

4. Remove drops of paint, glue, sheet rock mud, etc.

5. Wash the outside surface and dry it with a cleaning cloth so it shines. "Windex" type window cleaners work well here.

6. If you need to wash the inside, use a mild solution of all-purpose cleaner.

7. Never attempt to move appliances by dragging them—you'll scratch the floor.

Caution

Be careful not to do anything that might damage the slick, smooth, dirt and stain resistant surface of appliances. Enamel and porcelain are strong but they can't withstand scouring cleansers, steel wool, colored nylon scrub pads, etc. These will only leave a scratched, dull surface that's hard to clean forever after.

METAL

Most metal can be dusted, cleaned, and polished all in one step with fast-evaporating "Windex" type cleaner.

On tarnished metal use a gentle polish like Nevr Dull or Brasso. Some surfaces appear to be metal and are not. When metal polishing, I start or experiment in an inconspicuous place so if something is unpolishable I'll know before it's too late. Keep metal polishes of any kind off adjoining surfaces such as wood or cloth. That "black" that comes off when you're polishing is oxidation. Apply the polish or paste as per directions on the container and wipe with a cotton terry towel. Repeat until all the black goes and the metal glows!

Stainless and Chrome

It may be metal, but it's not indestructible and it is stain*less* (not un-stainable) steel. It will stain, just less than other metals. Also, chrome and stainless are not one and the same. Often we attempt to clean and polish stainless to match the attached chrome fixture and it cannot be done.

Stainless will need very little cleaning. Just wash and buff dry.

To give it a gleam, you can use a bit of stainless polish. However, new stainless seldom needs polish.

For chrome, just use "Windex" type window cleaner and wipe dry. Don't attack chrome with acid or abrasive cleansers—you'll dull or scratch it.

WOOD

Careful! You need to know if the finish is strong enough to keep out moisture. With wood, there is always a danger that water will penetrate the finish and raise the grain, or soften the glue on veneer. If the wood is varnished, clean with a damp cloth and mild solution of all-purpose cleaner,

just as you would Formica. Wipe the surface dry with a cleaning cloth. Never leave water standing on wood.

REMOVING
LABELS AND STICKERS

Labels are on just about everything these days, especially anything expensive. Some seem to be applied with a space glue that refuses to ever leave its original placement, or to have been brewed up by a mad scientist determined to defy all professional cleaners and their solutions.

All visible labels have to come off. This can take time and do damage that is very expensive.

There are two basic ways to get labels off: scrape them off or lift them chemically. Both methods work well in the right situations with the right procedures.

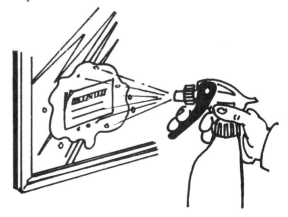

Before launching your offensive against a label, first try the kindergarten approach. Work your fingernail under one edge or corner of the label and see if you can slowly peel it off. There are a few reasonable scientists around who designed mastics that hold labels well in all weather and abuse, yet won't adhere permanently to the object and peel off perfectly.

1 st Choice:
Chemical Lift

There is some solvent that will dissolve most "stickum." Once the stickum is dissolved, the label or sticker loses its hold and slips off. Glass, plastic, cultured marbles, enamel, and varnished surfaces are pretty substantial, and 95% of the time you are safe taking the dissolving approach.

There are many solvents, and of course you always want one that will not harm or react with the surface in question. The best and safest solvent I've used overall is the citrus-based one called De-Solv-it®. It is oily, safe, and lifts most glues. Once you've applied it, work it under the edge of the label so it can attack and release the glue.

Once the label is removed, apply a bit more solvent and with a towel wipe the area of contact to remove any remaining residue. Then wash the entire area with all-purpose cleaner. Be careful of other solvents such as lacquer thinner and phosphoric acid.

Some solvents will liquefy carpet, plastic, etc.

2 nd Choice:
Ye Ol' Scraper

Get and use a <u>new</u> razor scraper (a scraper with a NEW blade in it). It doesn't matter what style, they all work. Just don't try to use a plain blade in your fingers.

1 Always wet the surface with a light soapy solution (like Joy and water) before you start. **Never scrape dry**!

2 Let solution sit on the label for a minute or two.

3 Scrape in one direction only—**forward**. Never go back and forth on a surface because if a piece of sand or grit gets caught under the blade on a backstroke it will cut or scratch the surface.

4 If the label is "tough," work it slow. Don't bully it off. The razor will cut what it can at its own speed.

5 Keep the surface WET! This will lubricate it and prevent damage.

6 While you're working, keep the lid on any solvent and cover the razor blade when it's not in use. Both can hurt people and places and there goes your time and profit, not to mention your peace of mind.

7 When you're done, wipe the surface clean.

8 Now, contain those removed labels! 80% of workers will flip a dead label onto the floor or into the air, but ah—it lives again as it dries and sticks to carpets, floors, shoes, equipment, and the inside of waste containers. It can take just as long to remove a label the second time. Grab a piece of that paper towel you used to wipe the surface dry with and wrap the removed, but still sticky, label in the paper

towel and then drop it in the trash. This should put it out of action.

PAINT REMOVAL

Even the most meticulous painter will leave a few drops, some smears and splashes and overspray that they didn't see, that no one saw, but the owner will spot instantly (after the dust is gone).

By the time you get to it, paint is usually set up and hard, so paint thinner won't touch it. Occasionally, if it is semi-fresh, thinner will re-emulsify it so it can be removed.

On slick hard surfaces use a razor blade scraper. It will also pop the droplets nicely off of textured hard surfaces. Be sure to wet the surface first and be careful scraping (often the fresh new coat of paint comes off easily, too).

The above approaches work well on masonry, too.

In carpet, dried droplets can be pinched with pliers, or the like, to crush them and break them up. Or, trim the spot with fingernail clippers if it is a napped type fabric.

Touching the spot with a bit of paint remover on the end of a Q-tip can break down a drop of oil-base paint and then a cloth with paint thinner on it will usually pull it out of the carpet. If the dried drip is water-base paint, use a remover like Goof Off.

SHEET ROCK MUD
Drops and Drips

Are water soluble, so just wet them and wait, then wipe.

GLUE

Everyone uses glue now—contact cement, carpet mastic, construction adhesive, etc., and if tiny bits of glue are left around we usually take care of it. If there is a LOT of misplaced glue around (like smeared up walls, etc.) turn it back to the contractor.

If it is just a small amount:

1. Try carefully clipping it out of carpet with nail clippers, or shattering it with pliers and then vacuuming it up. Once dry and hard, glue is usually brittle.

2. On surfaces, see if you can pop it off with a plastic scraper.

3. Often a careful application of

solvents like lacquer thinner, De-Solv-it®, or nail polish remover will bring glue back to its soft state and it can be wiped up and absorbed with a towel.

> **CAUTION: Anything strong enough to melt glue will melt other things! Always test first.**

SPOT & STAIN
Smarts

Your job here has two parts: Not just removal, but PREVENTION!

Prevention

If stains don't occur, you won't have to worry about them. And you CAN help prevent them:

- Keep good mats or dropcloths in critical catch-all areas!

- Control the circulation and disposal of food and drink.

- Police and remove spillables before they spill!

- Provide easy access to cleaning tools so "spillers" can clean it right up.

- Have extra protection and covers (mats, tarps, dropcloths) for potentially messy operations.

Removal

1. Act fast and catch it while it's fresh; chances for removal are 75% better. Remember: a spot is ON; a stain is IN!

2. Do all you can to identify the stain before you start: a) look, b) smell, c) ask, d) touch (but don't taste).

3. First blot up all the liquid and scrape up all the solids you can. A bone or plastic scraper is good for this and easy to carry right on you at all times. On a large liquid spill you can

use a wet/dry vacuum. Be careful not to spread the stain.

4. Use white cloths for stain removal. This tells you a) if the item is colorfast b) if the stain is coming out!

5. Pre-test any chemical you intend to use in a hidden area to make sure it won't discolor, damage, or dissolve the surface!

6. Apply the recommended spotter and work from the outside of the stain toward the inside, to avoid spreading the stain.

7. If it's a mystery stain, first try a dry solvent. If the stain remains, try a water-based spot remover.

8. Rinse chemical spotters out with water, blot the area dry and feather the edges. Brush or fluff up pile or nap.

9. On carpet and upholstery, put a thick pad of toweling over the spot, weigh it down with a heavy object, and leave it there for several hours to "wick up" any remaining moisture or stain residue that may still be there deep down.

Basic Spot Summary

This is a basic chart of "dissolvers" I use to be sure I'm using the right solvent on the right stain. Some stains do require a combination of chemicals and a several-stage attack.

For a good general background in stain removal and a great reference book, I recommend **The Stainbuster's Bible**. For a copy send $13.95 plus $3.25 for postage to:

Stainbuster's Bible
PO Box 700
Pocatello ID 83204

General Rule of Thumb

Dry Solvent	Acid Spotter	Alkaline Spotter
lipstick	(most vegetable and	(most stains of animal
mascara	plant stains)	origin)
blusher	mustard	protein
other cosmetics	grass	blood
shoe polish	soft drinks	sweat
nail polish	fruit juice	urine
lacquer	wine	vomit
enamel	whiskey	animal or human waste
airplane glue	medicine	other body discharges
ink	coffee	albumin
paint	tea	egg
varnish	soy sauce	other foods
tar	steak sauce	milk
oil	cherry pie	starch
carbon	tree bark	sweets
crayons	chocolate	glue
pencil	mud	beer
wax	tannin	red dye
smoke stains		ice cream

TRASH & DEBRIS

You'll wonder where it all comes from, how something brand new can end up with more left over than was installed!

Construction sites actually generate trash. Such as:

lunch wrappers
beverage cans
cigarette butts
material scraps
styrofoam and other padding/
    packaging
strapping/wrapping
broken articles
misfit units
crates
leftover everything
    (imagine the leftovers of 15 subs!)

And amazingly, most everyone on the scene (no matter how upright and moral they may otherwise be) have been "cleaned up after" most of their lives, so the second they are finished with waste/trash/scraps or garbage, it becomes public domain, the property of the cleanup crew (you). Equally amazing is how long it can take to pick up all this!

Consider all this stuff now—lying all over, wet, half buried or stuck to things, unmarked, sharp, heavy, perhaps poisonous, and you have a big job, often not figured in the bid.

Here are some of the concerns you will have here:

Things in the way

a. New material

b. Leftover material

c. Scraps and trash

d. Trash getting recirculated into your completed areas

Bins and containers

a. Are always full

b. Are inadequate or dangerous

HAVE A
TRASH AGREEMENT

Have a clear (and spelled out in detail) understanding with your client about trash handling. The contractor may have you haul debris after different phases of construction. For example you may make a "sweep" after framing is complete. All framing debris is cleaned from the interior and the floor swept, leaving the area clean for the next construction phase.

One of three things is done with the debris:

1. Put it in a pile on the exterior for a future "haul away."

2. Put it in a pile, load it onto a dump truck, and haul it away now.

3. Put it into a dumpster which is periodically emptied by a commercial garbage removal firm.

Pirating of "leftovers" by employees

Allow no pirating! When construction people seem to "toss" a perfectly good piece of sheet rock, a faulty fixture, a roll of wire, a scrap of insulation, a piece of firewood, we may be tempted almost beyond our limits to "take it home."

DON'T! Trash robbing causes a bad image and a loss of time as your crew argues over the spoils! You won't believe how much trouble you can get in deciding what to do with a reject sink left on the job.

One good way to prevent all this is to arrange to provide, for the contractor, a worker from 4-8 hours a day on a regular basis to clean up behind the various trades and keep debris moved to the dumpster or hauled away.

A FINE FINISH!

Good construction cleanup jobs and good books have to end… and move on to more of the same, hopefully more fun and more profit.

We've covered about a hundred dos and at least as many don'ts for any construction cleanup job. Read them again if you must, but DON'T IGNORE THEM. They all count. One violation—one doing of one "don't"—can kill a whole job. This big job DONE WELL is only a bunch of little jobs DONE WELL.

When you first read through all this, construction cleanup might sound a little intimidating, but it isn't. One or two jobs and all of those dos, don'ts, lists, and rules will fall into place, and like driving a car, will come easy… as long as you watch the ROAD!

Construction cleanup is a special slot in the cleaning world, a specialized division of the cleaning profession. Not many of us are in it, but with patience, and cultivation of skills and clients you can and will build a good, solid business single-handedly (just yourself) or with a crew. You'll know after a few jobs whether you like it or not and if you like it, there is much more around, more coming.

Just remember to:

1. Do good work
2. Keep good records (before, during, after)
3. Keep focused on "construction cleanup"
4. And keep everyone HAPPY!

You'll become one of the more satisfied and rewarded professionals in the cleaning field.

Good Cleaning,

Don Aslett

P.S. As you finish up a job, start checking, if you haven't already, on who is going to do the regular janitorial work after the facility is in full operation. By now, you probably know the owners and they know you. This is a perfect time to line up some additional work.

Your Own

CLEANING BUSINESS

Cleaning up is big business. It continues to be a growing industry, one that offers good income and a secure future to those who can do and manage the work effectively and have the will to succeed.

Cleaning is also one of the easiest fields to enter. It requires very little start-up capital, yields an amazing 30% average return on investment, and offers the kind of life that will satisfy the dreams and needs of many who have been thinking of starting a business of their own: freedom of choice, attractive income potential, no special educational requirements, tax advantages, opportunities everywhere, and

Cleaning Up for a Living
by
Don Aslett &
Mark Browning

208 pages illustrated; $39.95

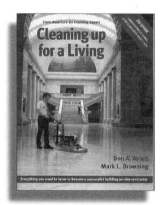

the chance to branch out into numerous related careers.

In **Construction Cleanup** you've been introduced to one of the many exciting specialties in the profession. If you want to go on to explore the whole constellation of cleaning industry opportunities, and make sure that any you choose turn out a success for you, **Cleaning Up For a Living** is the book you want next.

It's a complete, comprehensive, step-by-step guide to everything you'll ever need to know about the business. It's written in a down-to-earth, lively style that makes even the most "technical" subject easy to grasp and understand, and includes 34 pages of blank forms of all kinds you can just photocopy and use.

Be a
PROFESSIONAL!

"Sometimes it's a jungle out there for all of us janitors, being in a profession where the public 'expects the positive and reports the negative.' We do our share of hacking through the underbrush of complaints as we clean up after what seem like some unique wild animals. But our profession, the cleaning profession, is the first and oldest—and I believe the best—in the world, especially when we learn to enjoy it, and use it to serve mankind. Here is a manual written just for cleaning people by a fellow cleaner. This book will give you insight, inspiration, and some new angles to do the job at hand faster and better while loving every minute of it."

The most comprehensive training manual ever for the frontline cleaner. You will learn here, from a master, not merely how to clean, but all the hidden and equally important "people" skills.

Don Aslett founded Varsity Contractors, Inc., a total facility services firm, more than fifty years ago. The wisdom and knowledge of Don and all of his Varsity managers, supervisors, and cleaning crews is boiled down here in *The Professional Cleaner's Personal Handbook*.

The first half of the book provides all of the important background information every cleaner needs. It begins by putting the cleaning profession into perspective, explaining the position of pride and responsibility it unquestionably is. Among the many topics it goes on from there to cover are: safety, how to care for your equipment, professional ethics, how to get clients and coworkers to like you, how to avoid the pitfalls and cope with the doldrums of the cleaning career, how to assess your own performance, how to handle the wide, wild world of "what ifs" (unexpected, unusual, and "emergency" things) that crop up every day and week, and how to further your career in cleaning. The second half of the book is the actual "how-to" of cleaning, including how to organize yourself and your crew.

The Professional Cleaner's Personal Handbook,

200 pages illustrated;
$19.95

Be a Cleaner
THROUGH & THROUGH

❝ It's easy to teach people cleaning techniques, but it's hard to teach and convince them to have a good attitude about it. As America's Number One Cleaning Expert and someone who built a $250 million cleaning company from scratch on the strength of the enthusiasm and excellence of its employees, I've written this book to help you implement a motivation campaign for your janitors.

Motivation has to come from within, it can't just be external expressions— awards, or trinkets, or a new piece of equipment every few years. Morale building and motivation comes from actions, not talk and thank-you speeches.

I have firsthand, frontline experience of what really works, and what doesn't when it comes to encouraging your custodians. ❞

From the man who has employed 40,000 janitors comes a book devoted to job enrichment for the cleaning ranks. Don Aslett is the founder and chairman of the board of Varsity Contractors, Inc., a total facility maintenance firm operating in sixteen states.

Managing cleaning crews for forty years has given Aslett insights into what makes cleaners tick. **How to Upgrade and Motivate Your Cleaning Crews** shares hundreds of ways to uplift the image of "the cleaner" and motivate crews to take pride in their work.

How to Upgrade and Motivate Your Cleaning Crews

128 pages illustrated; $19.95

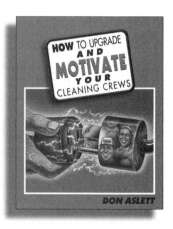

Other Aslett books you won't want to miss...

The Brighter Side of the Broom

200 pp, illustrated; $16.95

You'll celebrate, laugh, and grow with this humorously detailed book of funny janitor stories filled with business misadventures and triumphs.

From drunken crows to outhouse escapades on the slopes of Sun Valley, Don's adventures will leave you laughing while encouraging you to persevere and never give up. In his fifty year quest of expanding his cleaning business across America, you'll learn that you don't have to start out as the best to be the best. Don has grown from an ambitious small town janitor to a media celebrity and bestselling author.

This collection of stories expresses Don's philosophy of being honest with customers, having courage to take on challenging projects, and providing the service you agreed to perform even in the midst of unforeseen circumstances.

Reading this will lift your spirits and enhance your business.

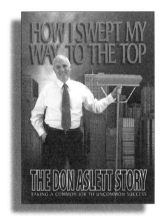

How I Swept My Way to the Top: The Don Aslett Story

576 pp, 100s of photos; $24.95

From Outhouse to Penthouse— how America's #1 Cleaning Expert made millions by cleaning toilets. Following is an excerpt from Don's autobiography on "Starting my biz."

Growing up on a farm in Southeast Idaho, my parents, and most of my other relatives and neighbors were people who worked for themselves, farmers and other entrepreneurs. My own teenage farming ventures, too, soon put enough money in the bank to pay for a move to college.

All went well for a while in my new university existence until I began to realize that the many free privileges I enjoyed at home like plenty of food, a car, room, and washing and ironing services, did not exist at school. It was cash on the line. I never imagined how fast my wheat money would scatter in the wind of expenses. I could see that it wouldn't be long until my hog, bull, and hay savings would be gone, too. I didn't expect anyone to pay my way, so for the first time in my life (and the last, by the way), I went looking for a job.

Previously my brothers and I had people ask us to work for them. Here, no one knew me and I was just another college boy looking for a part-time job. I concentrated on the commercial and industrial section of town, and finally landed a job at a soda pop-bottling factory, starting wage seventy-five cents an hour.

The machinery was old and it constantly broke bottles, the mixer leaked oil into the syrup, and the calibration for dispensing the syrup was always out of adjustment, which resulted in inconsistent batches. Kicking the machinery was part of policy and procedure to keep it running. Within a week, my roommate and I could run the entire operation (washing the bottles, filling and capping them, and loading them on a truck). Good thing, too, because the owner would turn the place over to us and disappear goose hunting for days. Every day was an adventure here, and I was cured of ever being a pop drinker after finding dead mice, bugs, twigs, and other things in the pop under the inspection light.

Payday came at the end of the month, and my 90 hours at seventy-five cents an hour equaled $67.50. The owner handed me a check for a little over forty dollars. Sure I had been cheated, I threw it down on his beverage-stained old wood desk and said, "What are these FICA, Federal, State, and Local 64 deductions? I want my money!"

"Those are things we have to take out," he said.

"Not out of my check, you don't!" I gave him back the keys to the door, grabbed my sadly reduced check, and walked out, determined to eventually work for myself.

This time I went to the college career office and talked to the director of the department, who after listening to the story of my poor pop-bottling payoff said, "Well then, you need to start your own business. People call all the time for help with yard work and housecleaning." I instantly recognized the opportunity and envisioned the market. When I came home that night I sat down with my roommate Marvin and proposed that we go into business together. We agreed to do it and included another roommate, Johnny Palleria, calling ourselves "The College Cleanup and Repair Team." This was a bold move for three young bachelors—up to that point, I had never even made a bed. I headed for the graphic arts department, where I designed and printed up our first brochure, then dropped several hundred copies off on doorsteps in the neighborhood…

Don't miss this remarkable rags to riches story—576 pages, call to order 208-232-3535.

Cleaning Novelties from Don Aslett

Prices subject to change, please call for current price sheet. **Phone Orders 208-232-3535.**

Show pride in your profession by sporting a **Squeegee Lapel Pin**. It's a great reward for the window washer in training. $1.95 each; $18 dozen.

Impressive, 4-color **Name Tags** that proclaim, "I am a Professional Cleaner." Come in gangs of four to run through your printer, or hand-letter. Actual size 3 7/8" x 2 5/8". Designed to use with squeegee lapel pin. $1.20/four; $3/dozen.

I am a Professional Cleaner

YOUR NAME

Toilet Soup or Hot Chocolate Mug

leaves no doubt at break time as to who you are and what you do for a living. $12.95 each.

Chocolate Outhouse!

Make eye-catching centerpieces and inexpensive door prizes and decorations with this reusable candy outhouse mold. $3.95 each.

Squirting Toilet.

I have one in my briefcase and I've even squirted governors, principals, and movie stars with it. Helps people realize that professional cleaners are people! $4.95 each.

What do the first place winners get? The coveted **Golden Outhouse Trophy**. What better prize at your special event! $18 each.

Carry a **Johnny Lip Light** (to inspect under the rim of the toilet); playfully scare people with the idea that you're going to use it. "I'm as good as any dentist (we both work in enamels!)." $3.95 each.

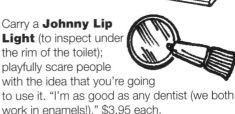

Found tags to get lost items safely back to their owners and let them know the names of the janitors that found them! .20 each; $2/dozen.

Colorful **Spot Removal Chart** makes a great giveaway for customers. Explains how to approach over 25 different stains. $1 each; $10/dozen; 100 or more 40¢ ea.

A Toilet Cleaner's Attitude

A quick, motivational read about Don's experiences cleaning the Sun Valley Ski Resort early in his career. 36 pages; $2.95 each.

CLEANING – New Editions!

HELP! Around the House
A Mother's Guide to Getting the Family to Pitch in and Clean Up
DON ASLETT
NEW Book!

IS THERE LIFE AFTER HOUSEWORK?
A Revolutionary Approach to Cutting Your Cleaning Time by 75%
DON ASLETT
2nd Edition

PET CLEAN-UP MADE EASY
Tackle any pet mess, any time, in a snap—from stains and smells to fleas and furballs
DON ASLETT
2nd Edition

DO I DUST OR VACUUM FIRST?
Answers to the 100 toughest, most frequently asked questions about housecleaning
DON ASLETT
2nd Edition

MAKE YOUR HOUSE DO THE HOUSEWORK
DON ASLETT

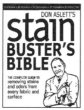

DON ASLETT'S stain BUSTER'S BIBLE
THE COMPLETE GUIDE to removing stains and odors from every fabric and surface
DON ASLETT
LAURA ASLETT SIMONS

The Guide to HARD WOOD FLOOR Care & Maintenance
GRANT ASLETT

DON ASLETT
NO TIME TO CLEAN!
HOW TO REDUCE & PREVENT CLEANING THE PROFESSIONAL WAY

The CLEANING ENCYCLOPEDIA
Your A to Z illustrated guide to cleaning like the pros!
Don Aslett
Don Aslett's CLEAN IN A MINUTE

WHO SAYS IT'S A WOMAN'S JOB TO CLEAN?
DON ASLETT

DECLUTTERING

WEEKEND MAKEOVER
Take Your Home from Messy to Magnificent in Only 48 Hours!
DON ASLETT
2nd Edition

CLUTTER'S LAST STAND
It's Time to De-Junk Your Life!
DON ASLETT
2nd Edition

THE OFFICE CLUTTER CURE
Get organized, get results!
DON ASLETT
2nd Edition

DON ASLETT'S CLUTTER FREE! Finally & Forever
2nd Edition

For Packrats Only
How to clean up, clear out and dejunk your life forever!
Don Aslett

AUDIO CD

DEJUNK LIVE!
with DON ASLETT

* Formerly *Lose 200 Lbs. This Weekend*

VIDEOS

Don Aslett's Video Seminar
Is There Life After Housework?

Don Aslett's CLEAN IN A MINUTE

Restroom Maintenance & Sanitation
VIDEO

PROFESSIONAL CLEANERS

Cleaning up for a Living
Don A. Aslett
Mark L. Browning

THE PROFESSIONAL CLEANER'S PERSONAL HANDBOOK
DON ASLETT

HOW TO UPGRADE AND MOTIVATE YOUR CLEANING CREWS
DON ASLETT

CONSTRUCTION CLEANUP
A GUIDE TO AN EXCITING AND PROFITABLE CLEANING SPECIALTY
DON ASLETT

CLIP ART CD

Don Aslett's Professional Cleaner's CLIP ART

THE BRIGHTER SIDE OF THE BROOM
FUNNY STORIES FROM AMERICA'S #1 CLEANING EXPERT

WRITING

Get Organized, Get Published!
225 Ways to Make Time for Success
Don Aslett and Carol Cartaino

HOW TO WRITE & SELL YOUR FIRST BOOK
Don Aslett

" My focus for years now has been on giving you more time by showing you how you can accomplish things better and faster. How to free yourself up so you can have more of what you really want out of life. My books are loaded with fresh, new, and down-to-earth solutions for getting 'it' all done, so you can move on to things that really matter to you. **"**

AUTOBIOGRAPHY!

BUSINESS & MISC.

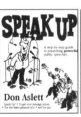 

** Formerly *How to Have a 48-Hour Day*

MAIL your order to:
  Don Aslett
  PO Box 700
  Pocatello ID 83204
CALL: 888-748-3535
      208-232-3535
FAX: 208-235-5481
ONLINE: www.Aslett.com

☐ Don, please put my name and the enclosed list of my friends on your mailing list for the **Clean Report** bulletin and catalog.

TITLE	Retail	Qty	Amt
Barnyard to Boardroom: Business Basics	$14.95		
Clean in a Minute	$6.95		
DVD Clean in a Minute	$14.99		
Cleaning Up for a Living (Revised)	$39.95		
Clutter Free! Finally & Forever	$12.99		
Clutter's Last Stand, 2nd Edition	$9.95		
Construction Cleanup	$19.95		
CD Dejunk LIVE! *Audio CD*	$14.99		
Don Aslett's Stainbuster's Bible	$13.95		
Done! (Formerly How to Have a 48-Hour Day)	$9.95		
Do I Dust Or Vacuum First? 2nd Edition	$9.95		
For Packrats Only	$13.95		
Get Organized, Get Published	$18.99		
HELP! How to get help around the House	$9.95		
How I Swept My Way to the Top	$24.99		
How to Be #1 With Your Boss	$9.99		
How to Handle 1,000 Things at Once	$12.99		
How to Upgrade & Motivate Your Cleaning Crew	$19.95		
How to Write & Sell Your First Book	$14.95		
Is There Life After Housework? 2nd Edition	$9.95		
DVD/VHS Is There Life After Housework?	$19.95		
Make Your House Do the Housework	$19.95		
No Time To Clean! (+ free color spot chart)	$12.99		
Painting Without Fainting	$9.99		
Pet Clean-Up Made Easy, 2nd Edition	$9.95		
CD Professional Cleaner's Clip Art	$29.95		
DVD Restroom Sanitation (with Quiz Booklet)	$69.95		
Speak Up (Don's guide to public speaking)	$12.99		
The Brighter Side of the Broom	16.95		
The Cleaning Encyclopedia	$16.95		
The Office Clutter Cure, 2nd Edition	$9.95		
The Professional Cleaner's Handbook	$19.95		
Weekend Makeover (Formerly Lose 200 Lbs...)	$9.95		
Who Says It's A Woman's Job to Clean?	$6.95		
Wood Floor Care	$9.95		

Shipping: $3.25 for first book or video plus 75¢ for each additional.		
	Subtotal	
	Idaho residents only add 5% Sales Tax	
	Shipping	
	TOTAL	

☐ Check enclosed   ☐ Visa   ☐ MasterCard   ☐ Discover   ☐ AmEx

Card No. _____ CVV _____

Exp. Date _____ Phone _____

Signature X _____
Ship to:
Your Name _____

Street Address _____

City ST Zip _____

CLEANING – New Editions!

 **HELP! Around the House** — *A Mother's Guide to Getting the Family to Pitch in and Clean Up* — DON ASLETT — NEW Book!

 **IS THERE LIFE AFTER HOUSEWORK?** — *A Revolutionary Approach to Cutting Your Cleaning Time by 75%* — DON ASLETT — 2nd Edition

 **PET CLEAN-UP MADE EASY** — Tackle any pet mess, any time, in a snap — from stains and smells to fleas and furballs — DON ASLETT — 2nd Edition

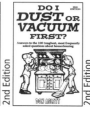 **DO I DUST OR VACUUM FIRST?** — Answers to the 100 toughest, most frequently asked questions about housecleaning — DON ASLETT — 2nd Edition

 **MAKE YOUR HOUSE DO THE HOUSEWORK** — DON ASLETT

 DON ASLETT'S **stain BUSTER'S BIBLE** — The complete guide to removing stains and odors from every fabric and surface

 The Guide to **HARD WOOD FLOOR Care & Maintenance** — GRANT ASLETT

 DON ASLETT — **NO TIME TO CLEAN!** — HOW TO REDUCE & PREVENT CLEANING THE PROFESSIONAL WAY

 The **CLEANING ENCYCLOPEDIA** — Your A to Z Illustrated guide to cleaning like the pros! — Don Aslett — Don Aslett's **CLEAN IN A MINUTE**

 WHO SAYS IT'S A **WOMAN'S JOB TO CLEAN?** — DON ASLETT — America's #1 Cleaning Expert

DECLUTTERING

 **WEEKEND MAKEOVER** — Take Your Home from Messy to Magnificent in Only 48 Hours! — DON ASLETT — 2nd Edition *

 **CLUTTER'S LAST STAND** — It's Time to De-Junk Your Life! — DON ASLETT — 2nd Edition

 **THE OFFICE CLUTTER CURE** — Get organized, get results! — DON ASLETT — 2nd Edition

 DON ASLETT'S **CLUTTER FREE! Finally & Forever** — Including true confessions & solutions from 100's of your fellow packrats!

 For Packrats Only — How to clean up, clear out and dejunk your life forever! — Don Aslett, author of No Time to Clean and Clutter's Last Stand

AUDIO CD

 **DEJUNK LIVE!** WITH DON ASLETT

* Formerly *Lose 200 Lbs. This Weekend*

VIDEOS

 95 Entertainment-Packed Minutes! **Don Aslett's Video Seminar Is There Life After Housework?** — Don Aslett's **CLEAN IN A MINUTE** — **Restroom** Maintenance & Sanitation VIDEO

PROFESSIONAL CLEANERS

 Don Aslett's #1 Cleaning Expert **Cleaning up for a Living** — Don A. Aslett, Mark L. Browning

 **THE PROFESSIONAL CLEANER'S PERSONAL HANDBOOK** — DON ASLETT

 **HOW TO UPGRADE AND MOTIVATE YOUR CLEANING CREWS** — DON ASLETT

 **CONSTRUCTION CLEANUP** — A GUIDE TO AN EXCITING AND PROFITABLE CLEANING SPECIALTY — DON ASLETT

CLIP ART CD

 Don Aslett's Professional Cleaner's **CLIP ART**

 **THE BRIGHTER SIDE OF THE BROOM** — FUNNY STORIES FROM AMERICA'S #1 CLEANING EXPERT — DON ASLETT

WRITING

 **Get Organized, Get Published!** — 225 WAYS TO MAKE TIME FOR SUCCESS — Don Aslett and Carol Cartaino

 HOW TO WRITE & SELL YOUR FIRST BOOK — Don Aslett

> My focus for years now has been on giving you more time by showing you how you can accomplish things better and faster. How to free yourself up so you can have more of what you really want out of life. My books are loaded with fresh, new, and down-to-earth solutions for getting 'it' all done, so you can move on to things that really matter to you.